the Virtuous Woman

Other books by Vicki Courtney from Broadman & Holman

Your Girl: Raising a Godly Daughter in an Ungodly World

Yada Yada: A Devotional Journal for Moms

More Than Just Talk: A Journal for Girls

∾∾∾

Author Web sites to check out

www.vickicourtney.com—to view Vicki Courtney's current speaking schedule or to find information about inviting her to speak.

www.virtuousreality.com—features online magazines for preteen, teen, college, and adult women.

www.virtuousreality.com/events—provides a schedule of upcoming Yada Yada and Yada Yada Junior events for girls ages third through twelfth grades and mothers; also information about how you can bring an event to your area.

www.virtuepledge.com—features an online community where girls and young women can pledge themselves to biblical virtue.

the Virtuous Woman

Woman

shattering the superwoman myth

Vicki · Courtney

BROADMAN
&HOLMAN
PUBLISHERS

NASHVILLE, TENNESSEE

0-8054-3054-7

Published by Broadman & Holman Publishers
Nashville, Tennessee

Unless otherwise noted, Scripture quotations are
from the Holy Bible, NIV, New International Version,
copyright © 1973, 1978, 1984 by International Bible
Society. Other versions include: NLT, New Living
Translation, copyright © 1996. Used by permission of
Tyndale House Publishers, Inc., Wheaton, IL 60189 USA.
All rights reserved.; *The Message,* the New Testament in
Contemporary English, © 1993 by Eugene H. Peterson,
published by NavPress, Colorado Springs, Colo.;
and KJV, King James Version.

This book is dedicated to the memory of my grandmother, Luna Moore. Her devotion to godly virtue was not lost on this granddaughter.

Acknowledgments

To my husband, Keith, and children, Ryan, Paige, and Hayden: Thank you for your patience during times when I fall woefully short in my calling as a wife and mother. It is my deepest desire to consistently live out the truths contained in the book.

To two of my greatest influencers in ministry and all-time favorite virtuous women:

Ada Ferguson: Thank you for the time you invested in my life, not to mention the lives of countless others. I will forever treasure the memories of sitting around your kitchen table with other young mothers and soaking up your godly wisdom. We were a tough group, and I am sure at times you must have wondered if you were wasting your time. You were not! You are a godly role model, mentor, and most of all, friend.

Barbara O'Chester: Out of obedience to the Lord and a desire to reach women, what you started as a women's retreat in your local church in 1969 to reach thirty-five women grew to reach tens of thousands of women across the country for more than three decades. As the founder of Great Hill's Retreat Ministry, you were doing women's events long before they became a formal concept. You are truly a pioneer in women's ministry. In 1995 you took a chance on me and asked me to join your team as a workshop teacher. Three years of traveling with your ministry and being surrounded by some of the godliest women of our time has molded me into who I am today. God used you and Great Hill's Retreat Ministry as an inspiration to begin Virtuous Reality Ministries. Your legacy continues. You will never know this side of heaven the countless lives that have been changed, mine included, as a result of your obedience.

Contents

Who can find a virtuous woman? for her price is far above rubies. The heart of her husband doth safely trust in her, so that he shall have no need of spoil. She will do him good and not evil all the days of her life. She seeketh wool, and flax, and worketh willingly with her hands. She is like the merchants' ships; she bringeth her food from afar. She riseth also while it is yet night, and giveth meat to her household, and a portion to her maidens. She considereth a field, and buyeth it: with the fruit of her hands she planteth a vineyard. She girdeth her loins with strength, and strengtheneth her arms. She perceiveth that her merchandise is good: her candle goeth not out by night. She layeth her hands to the spindle, and her hands hold the distaff. She stretcheth out her hand to the poor; yea, she reacheth forth her hands to the needy. She is not afraid of the snow for her household: for all her household are clothed with scarlet. She maketh herself coverings of tapestry; her clothing is silk and purple. Her husband is known in the gates, when he sitteth among the elders of the land. She maketh fine linen, and selleth it; and delivereth girdles unto the merchant. Strength and honour are her clothing; and she shall rejoice in time to come. She openeth her mouth with wisdom; and in her tongue is the law of kindness. She looketh well to the ways of her household, and eateth not the bread of idleness. Her children arise up, and call her blessed; her husband also, and he praiseth her. Many daughters have done virtuously, but thou excellest them all. Favour is deceitful, and beauty is vain: but a woman that feareth the LORD, she shall be praised. Give her of the fruit of her hands; and let her own works praise her in the gates. (Prov. 31:10–31 KJV)

Introduction

I remember my first encounter with the renowned Proverbs 31 woman. I was a new believer and a new bride to boot. I had heard that when it comes to a biblical version of the "ideal woman," this was the gal to emulate. So I opened up my Bible and read the passage—all twenty-two verses in one sitting. Talk about overwhelming. I mean, somebody give this woman a chill pill, and make it fast! Just make sure she washes it down with some decaf. Just reading about her made me want to take a nap. If the formula for becoming virtuous was contained in these twenty-two verses, I was in big trouble, especially if it was meant to be interpreted in a literal sense.

I have no problem bringing my food from afar, whether it's take-out pizza or the bag-o-burgers deal at Sonic. I was thrilled to find the verse about the maidens and was quick to point it out to my husband. He responded by pointing out the sewing and cooking verses. Ouch. I'll have to pass on planting a vineyard until I can manage to keep a Chia pet alive. As for strengthening her arms, does this mean I can get a personal trainer to help me strengtheneth mine? If my husband's pants need hemming, can I hire someone else to layeth hands to the spindle and still get credit? Can I stretch out my hand to the poor by participating in the canned food drive at my kid's school? I don't care much for wearing purple and silks, but we definitely share a passion for finding the perfect outfit. When it comes to exhibiting the law of kindness, can there be exemptions on days when the toilets need cleaning, the kids are fighting, and I have PMS? Is my Sunday afternoon nap considered the bread of idleness? Did her husband and children rise up and call her blessed *every* day? I have a couple of teenagers who might rise up and call me "dorky," but "blessed" is pushing it. If beauty is vain, can every day be baggy-sweatpants-and-sloppy-ponytail day?

I wish I could tell you that reading the passage served as a turning point in my life, that I committed to follow in the footsteps of the Proverbs 31 woman from that day forward. Not so. I made a note to self: *Never, ever, read this passage again.* As far as I was concerned, it should come with a required warning label:

Caution: Reading this passage can induce more guilt than eating a one-pound bag of M&Ms. Common side effects include uncontrollable laughter, fatigue, shortness of breath, feelings of inadequacy, depression, and an irrepressible desire to pop this lady upside the head should you ever meet her. Read at your own risk.

And then it happened. Years later, a publisher asked me to write a Bible study for college women. As a speaker to women of all ages, I was growing more and more concerned about our culture's brand of the "ideal woman" and the resulting fallout it was producing in the lives of women, both Christian and non-Christian alike. I knew I wanted to write a study that would contrast the world's version of the ideal woman to God's version. Therefore I petitioned God to show me the ideal woman in his eyes. You got it—he took me right back to Proverbs 31. I begged and pleaded: *Please, Lord—don't make me write about Little Miss Perfect! Women are afraid of her! No one will buy the study!* But it was no use. Who was I to argue with God?

As I began researching different commentaries of the Proverbs 31 passage, I made a startling discovery: several commentaries speculate that the passage does not reference one actual woman; rather, it is a compilation of qualities that make up a virtuous woman. *Whew, what a relief! Santa Claus, the Tooth Fairy, and the Proverbs 31 woman— all in the same category: MAKE-BELIEVE!* Maybe she would have a more favorable reception if she left behind gifts and money like the first two. Instead, she leaves behind a big dose of guilt. Regardless, this new revelation changed my outlook and made reading the passage more palatable.

Now before you jump the gun and think we're off the hook, the purpose of the passage, regardless of whether this woman is real or an ideal, remains the same: *to assist women by providing a summary of what constitutes a virtuous woman.* In addition, it is meant to provide a quick reference guide to aid men in finding a noble wife.

After writing the Bible study about the Proverbs 31 woman for college women, followed by another study for women, I discovered that in spite of the intimidation factor, many women are curious about the Proverbs 31 woman. This passage is perhaps the single greatest text in the Bible addressing what it is to be the ideal woman in the eyes of God. Unfortunately, many women fail to give it a chance because they misunderstand the message behind the passage and get sidetracked by this woman's long and unattainable list of domestic accomplishments.

In this book we will look at the passage in practical terms and learn how best to apply it to our lives. Before we rush out to tillith our backyard and planteth a vineyard in an attempt to reach "virtuous" status, we'll take a look at what she was like on the *inside*.

I am excited that you have chosen to join me in this journey to better understand the Proverbs 31 woman. However, before we get started, I must make a disclaimer. I am not writing this book as an *authority* on the virtuous woman but rather as a *fellow sojourner*. If you are looking for a how-to manual on domesticity written by a woman who has it all together in the "virtue" department, this is not your book, and I am not your gal. I am no different from the majority of women—I get cranky with phone solicitors who call during the dinner hour, and my driving has not yet merited placing a fish on my car. I don't sew my own clothes or make biscuits from scratch. In fact, if the truth be told, I can hardly sew on a button, and I have a special fondness for heat-and-serve skillet dinners.

Regardless, I am intrigued by the Proverbs 31 passage and the challenge to be a woman who excels them all. Who doesn't want her husband and children to rise up and call her blessed? However incredible that sounds, our greatest motivator should be to please our Father. If the virtuous woman of Proverbs 31 is the ideal woman in God's eyes, I want to be like her with every ounce of my being. Who knows, in the end we might be surprised to discover that we had much more in common with the Proverbs 31 woman than we originally thought.

Who Can Find a Virtuous Woman?

Chapter 1

One glance at a rack of fashion magazines at the supermarket checkout certainly merits the question, Who can find a virtuous woman? In fact, the subtitles alone promote an anything-but-virtuous way of life for today's twenty-first-century woman. The decadent influence of the sexual revolution is apparent with subtitles such as "How to Satisfy the Naughty Male Needs," "Lust Lessons," "Leave Him Screaming for More," or "Get a Better Body—for Sex." Clearly these magazines operate under the assumption that women will shell out $3.50 an issue to find out what it takes to be the ideal woman in the eyes of men. Unfortunately, they assumed right. Problem is, the definition keeps changing. Prior to the 1960s, the ideal woman was demure, domestic, and for the most part, a homemaker whose life calling was to care for her husband and children. Picture June Cleaver here, pulling fresh-baked cookies from the oven as her children bounded through the door after school. Decked out in a dainty frock, pearls, and perfectly coifed hair, she was the picture of domesticity—a real dream-come-true for any man. She was the ideal woman of her day.

Fast-forward to today. On the heels of the sexual revolution and the radical women's liberation movement, we find that the ideal woman has traded her apron for low-waist jeans and cleavage-baring blouses. The old adage, "The way to a man's heart is through his stomach," seems to have been replaced with, "The way to a man's heart is by showing your stomach, and then some." Ah, but you say this is not what men *really* want and that deep down inside they still want the 1950s prototype of the ideal wife. I'm not so sure. In a survey of single, professional men, 44 percent claimed they would not even consider marrying a woman unless she was willing to live together first. My, how times have changed. One can only wonder what the same survey would yield in fifty more years.

How we define the ideal woman starts when we are young. For many, exposure to the world's definition of the ideal woman began at home. Some women were told to look pretty, lose weight, make straight A's, and pursue an education that would lend itself to making a good living. Others were exposed to parents living at breakneck speed to prove themselves to a world they couldn't really please. I'm afraid only a few had the good fortune to receive training on what it is to be a virtuous woman.

Even if parents do their best to stress virtuous qualities, children discover the qualities the world applauds. The world is loud and clear about the ideal woman. The media, magazines, the movie industry, and other outside influences bombard us with their opinions of the ideal woman.

You could probably fill a book with messages you received during your early years.

- Lose weight.
- Assert yourself.
- Don't be pushy.
- Be smart.
- Don't be too smart.
- Don't be a show-off.
- Never ask for what you want.
- Speak your mind.
- Guys won't like you if you _____.
- Guys won't like you unless you _____.

Sometimes the messages can be so contradictory they tie us in knots. No matter what we do, it's never enough. How can we reach a goal when the rules keep changing?

> *Am I now trying to win the approval of men, or of God? Or am I trying to please men? If I were still trying to please men, I would not be a servant of Christ.* (Gal. 1:10)

The Ideal Woman According to the World

I'm sure you have a concept of the world's definition of the ideal woman, but have you ever put it into words? Before we can look at God's definition of the ideal woman, we must first identify the world's definition to see if it hasn't influenced our way of thinking.

I realize that the definition will vary from person to person, but if you were to poll the general population, she might be like this:

> The ideal woman is independent, confident, and self-reliant. She is up-to-date with the latest fashions (all, of course, in a perfect size 4) and

dons a to-die-for haircut that screams "sassy!"
She has established herself in her job. She is professional and assertive, while at the same time,
witty and personable. Her savvy skills enable her
to charm potential clients and wow everyone
with whom she comes in contact. She can manage a career and a family. She is superwoman.
She does it all and she does it well. She is able to
manage the housework without getting frazzled
and make sure dinner is on the table by the time
her charming husband walks through the door.
She is attentive to his needs and never complains
about his annoying habit of channel surfing. Of
course, she is a tiger in the bedroom, having
gleaned her knowledge from the latest fashion
magazines. Her husband is proud of his trophy
bride who exercises daily and has a figure to
prove it. When it comes to being a mom, she is
at soccer games with her laptop and PTA meetings with her cell phone. She always looks polished and never seems tired. She takes off work
to drive on field trips or run cupcakes up to the
school on her child's birthday. Her children
adore her and share their innermost thoughts
and dreams with her. They never complain if she
lacks time for them because they are proud of
her many accomplishments.

I can honestly tell you that in all my years of living,
I have never met a woman who has been successful in
meeting the above standard. Most women who attempt it
are in therapy and are popping Prozac like it's candy. Yet
the world continues to bombard women with messages

that focus on the pursuit of beauty, brains, and a great body.

Anyone who has read 1 Samuel 16 knows what God says about the futility of the world's way of thinking. This passage records the prophet's mission to anoint one of Jesse's sons as the future king of Israel. Not knowing which son was the anointed one, when Samuel saw Jesse's son Eliab, he thought, "Surely the LORD's anointed stands here before the LORD" (v. 6). Eliab was, no doubt, the modern-day equivalent of the latest Hollywood hunk, and he seemed to have "future king" written all over him. However, the Spirit of God quickly corrected the snap judgment with a principle all of us can apply to our thinking when it comes to the definition of the ideal woman: "'Do not consider his appearance or his height, for I have rejected him. The LORD does not look at the things man looks at. Man looks at the outward appearance, but the LORD looks at the heart'" (v. 7).

If we are honest, most of us would probably plead guilty to the same approach. We look at others and often judge ourselves in the same way. First Samuel 16:7 relates powerfully to our quest to become the world's ideal woman.

Have you bought into the world's obsession with outward appearance in any way? Think not? Try this exercise just to make sure: Stand in front of a full-length mirror in your swimsuit and say with confidence, "I am fearfully and wonderfully made; your works are wonderful" (Ps. 139:14). Gotcha!

Scripture challenges other components of the world's definition of the ideal woman. The world says we can trade in our skills, hard work, and looks to have it all. Jesus said: "What good will it be for a man if he gains the whole world, yet forfeits his soul? Or what can a man give in exchange for his soul?" (Matt. 16:26). The world says, "Follow this formula to be bright and beautiful and in control." The apostle Paul wrote, "The wisdom of this world is foolishness in God's sight" (1 Cor. 3:19a). The world says, "Play your cards right and you can have everything you want." John tells us, "Do not love the world or anything in the world. If anyone loves the world, the love of the Father is not in him. For everything in the world— the cravings of sinful man, the lust of his eyes and the boasting of what he has and does—comes not from the Father but from the world" (1 John 2:15–16). The world says, "Stuff will make you happy, and more stuff will make you even happier." Matthew 6:19–21 says, "Do not store up for yourselves treasures on earth, where moth and rust destroy, and where thieves break in and steal. But store up for yourselves treasures in heaven, where moth and rust do not destroy, and where thieves do not break in and steal. For where your treasure is, there your heart will be also." The world says that washboard abs and toned thighs are worth the countless hours you spend each week at the gym. Timothy reminds us that "physical training is of some value, but godliness has value for all things, holding promise for both the present life and the life to come" (1 Tim. 4:8).

Even if it were possible to measure up to the world's skewed thinking, we'd be guilty of climbing a ladder that, in the end, is leaning against the wrong wall. How sad that so many are wearing themselves out with the climb.

So what can we do about the flood of worldly influences that surround us? Fortunately, we don't have to be hapless victims of our culture. We can choose our response. Here are some possibilities:

- We could take the Amish route and withdraw from the world. Not a problem, unless you're attached to your microwave, cell phone, and Grande Lattes from Starbucks.
- We can take the route of many religious types and rail against the evils around us. Trouble is, who wants to be around someone who complains all the time without offering solutions?
- We can bury our heads in the sand and pretend that everything is OK. Counselors call this "denial" and would be happy to explain it to you for about ninety dollars per hour.
- We can take the "if you can't beat 'em, join 'em" route and conform ourselves to the world (or die trying). Think "ladder" here.
- Or we can choose to live by God's standard.

The Ideal Woman According to God

There is no mistaking that the ideal woman in the eyes of God is a virtuous woman. Fortunately, God has left us a definition of a virtuous woman in Proverbs 31:10–31. Amazingly, the passage is speculated to have been written by King Lemuel as he reflected on his mother's teaching regarding the type of wife he should seek. It is thought that the poem did not originate with King Lemuel's mother but rather was a freestanding poem that had been passed down for many generations for the purpose of aiding men in identifying an ideal wife, as well as giving women a formula for becoming the ideal wife. The twenty-two verses are in an acrostic format, with each verse beginning with consecutive letters of the Hebrew alphabet to aid in easy memorization. While at first glance the Proverbs 31 woman may appear to be an outdated fixture of the past, her character qualities stand the test of time. The passage is just as meaningful today as it was when it was originally written. Be reminded, "All Scripture is God-breathed and is useful for teaching, rebuking, correcting and training in righteousness" (2 Tim. 3:16).

Unfortunately, many Christian women shy away from this passage as they measure themselves up against her domestic resumé. I recently plugged the term *Proverbs 31* into an Internet search engine and was amazed at the number of references it identified. Many were home pages containing such things as recipes, gardening tips, sewing patterns, and parenting advice. Some were very enjoyable to read, while others were disturbing. One Internet site actually claimed that to be a virtuous woman you must cook, clean, sew, garden, and be a stay-at-home mother. Another made the point that you are out of God's will if you wear pants, short hair, or choose a method other than homeschooling to educate your children. If that were true, one, two, three strikes—I'm out! If the passage is to be taken literally, we're all in trouble. The Proverbs 31 woman didn't just sew; she made her own thread! ("She selects wool and flax and works with eager hands" [Prov. 31:13]). It is easy to come away assuming that the ideal woman in God's eyes is a Bible-toting Martha Stewart.

Does your definition of the ideal woman closely align with the outward actions of the Proverbs 31 woman? Maybe your comfort zone is the kitchen, and you're known for your flaky pie crusts. Maybe you just whipped up matching mother-daughter frocks for the church banquet that you planned from start to finish. Perhaps you just faux-finished all the walls in your house, and you grow all your own fruits and vegetables in your garden out back. Does it take these things to become the ideal woman? Don't be fooled into thinking virtue simply means a return to the kitchen. If you're like me, you come up woefully short when it comes to cooking, cleaning, gardening, and sewing. But the good news is that virtue runs much deeper than domestic abilities. Virtue must first begin in the heart. We desperately need to fill our hearts and minds with God's real standard to be a virtuous woman. I believe God intended the virtuous woman of Proverbs 31 for far more than to depress us. He wants us to explore who this woman was on the inside. What made her tick? What would she be like today?

As we begin to examine the passage in depth, keep in mind that even though the passage focuses on the ideal wife, it is still relevant to single women. Becoming a virtuous woman doesn't begin on our wedding day. I've heard it said, "You are who you've been becoming." If we are to become virtuous, we must begin today. The truth is, living up to the model of the virtuous woman in Proverbs 31 is as difficult as living up to the model of the world's ideal woman, if not more so. Developing the qualities that led to this woman's virtuous standing will be a process that takes place over time. I expect that I will still be striving to develop these qualities until I breathe my last breath.

Preparing for the Pursuit

I'll never forget a precious conversation my son, Ryan, had with one of his buddies when they were around ten years old. Ryan's friend said he had seen a survey of jobs and the average salary for each in an article in the newspaper. He told Ryan, "When I get out of college,

I'm going to find a job as a CEO. I don't know what they do, but they sure make a lot of money."

Becoming a virtuous woman is a similar pursuit. Many women want to reach this status, but few are willing to put forth the time and effort required. Becoming a virtuous woman is a lifelong journey. There is no such thing as a quick fix. Reading a book (even this one), joining a Bible study, or attending church regularly will not bring answers to all of life's problems. But growing a relationship with Jesus Christ through his Word will give us the answers we need when we need them.

It is very important that we begin this journey with the right attitude, or we could quickly become overwhelmed and discouraged. I know when I tend to sense I'm in over my head, I have a tendency to want to give up. Let's start the pursuit with the attitude that we're all in over our heads and that our God is a patient and loving God of grace and mercy who understands our plight. He doesn't expect perfection, nor does he expect overnight results. All he asks of us is that we have teachable spirits and receptive hearts. In Matthew 13:1–23, Jesus' parable about a farmer sowing seed contains a deeper teaching concerning the receptivity of the human heart. Many refer to the parable of the sower as the Scattered Seed Principle. It basically assumes that God puts forth his Word (the scattered seed), but only a fraction will fall onto good soil. In the pursuit to be a virtuous woman, the best results will come when our hearts are tilled and prepared to receive his Word. Yet in the end it will be our choice when it comes to having a receptive and teachable heart.

The four types of soil Jesus described in the parable provide us with a means to gauge the receptivity of our own hearts. So the parable challenges us in regard to the truths presented in Proverbs 31 and the pursuit to be virtuous. It leads us to ask, "What kind of soil am I?"

Before we look at the four types of soil Jesus described, let me make a disclaimer. The parable of the soils is often interpreted as possible responses to the good news of Jesus Christ in regard to the forgiveness of sins and eternal life. Studying the parable has left many a Christian questioning their salvation. God abhors legalism and would never intend to tie us up in knots wondering whether we were ever saved in the first place. It is counterproductive to his purposes. If we are in a tailspin of doubt regarding our salvation, we will be of little use to him when it comes to kingdom matters and pointing other wayward hearts in his direction. In looking at the parable of the soils, my goal is to address the receptivity of our own hearts specifically regarding the truths of the Proverbs 31 passage.

That having been said, if after looking at the parable it causes a seed of doubt to spring up regarding your own eternal standing, don't let the enemy try to confuse you. Go directly to Scriptures that teach about salvation (John 1:12; 3:16; Acts 16:31; Rom. 5:8–10, 18–20, 10:9–13; Eph. 2:1–10). If you want to know about whether you have security in your relationship with Christ, go to the places that deal with security (John 10:27–30; Eph. 1:13; Phil. 1:6; Heb. 6:1–6). Don't get sidetracked from what Jesus is teaching in this parable. The parable of the sower has one meaning that applies to us in many different situations. As with all of Jesus' parables, we need to diligently apply the truth he presents to our lives while being careful not to squeeze the message out of shape in the process.

When it comes to principles that aid in understanding Scripture, the same can be said for proverbs, including the Proverbs 31 passage. Dr. Adrian Rogers said, "If you turn proverbs into promises, you will lose your faith."[1] For example Proverbs 22:6 says: "Train a child in the way he should go, and when he is old he will not turn from it." Is that a promise? No, it's a proverb. A proverb is a general principle that when followed will usually produce the described result. If you train your child properly, does that mean he or she will automatically turn out right? No, because children have a will of their own.

My point is, guard against getting sidetracked with overanalyzing passages that were meant to provide a general truth. Proverbs should be interpreted as proverbs; parables should be interpreted as parables.

Whew, I feel much better now that we've settled that. Where were we? Ah yes, the receptivity of our hearts regarding the pursuit to be virtuous women. When Jesus first told the parable, his disciples didn't understand the meaning behind the farmer sowing seed. When they got the Master alone, they asked for an explanation. Jesus told them this:

> When anyone hears the message about the
> kingdom and does not understand it, the evil one
> comes and snatches away what was sown in his
> heart. This is the seed sown along the path. The
> one who received the seed that fell on rocky places
> is the man who hears the word and at once
> receives it with joy. But since he has no root, he
> lasts only a short time. When trouble or persecu-
> tion comes because of the word, he quickly falls
> away. The one who received the seed that fell
> among the thorns is the man who hears the word,
> but the worries of this life and the deceitfulness of
> wealth choke it, making it unfruitful. But the one

who received the seed that fell on good soil is the
man who hears the word and understands it. He
produces a crop, yielding a hundred, sixty or thirty
times what was sown. (Matt. 13:19–23)

The first type of soil was hard. Because the seed was
unable to penetrate the ground, it provided fast food for
an enemy on the run. Fortunately hard soil doesn't have
to stay hard. Part of the wonder and mystery of our mag-
nificent God is his willingness to go to great lengths to
soften the hardest of hearts. In fact, you may have a story
of how he has softened your own heart. As someone who
was at one time strongly opposed to Christianity, I know
firsthand the power of a mighty God who actively draws
even the hardest of hearts to his loving truths. Occasionally we may come across a truth in God's Word that
we initially resist applying to our lives. Scriptures pertaining to loving our enemies, tithing, submission, witnessing, dying to self, etc., don't always produce an initial
response of "Oh boy! I can't wait to do that!" For many
women, the Proverbs 31 passage is on that list. Therefore,
before we set out to understand and implement the truths
of Proverbs 31 in our lives, we must first agree that God's
Word is the authority in our lives.

The second type of soil, the rocky soil, initially seems
better off than the hard-packed earth represented by the
first soil. When rain falls on the rocky ground, the water
actually concentrates in the spots between the nonab-
sorbent rocks. As a result, the seed springs up faster in the
rocky soil than in the good soil. But the quick growth is
deceptive. The plants find no place to become rooted and
cannot survive the scorching of the sun. How many times
have we heard a powerful sermon at church, an anointed
speaker at the women's retreat, or read a timely word

from the Bible and vowed to make a change? Maybe we even came up with a plan to ensure that the dawning of the truth would become more than just a flutter of excitement in our hearts, that it would actually be translated into action. Despite our pure intentions, however, sometimes the plans never came to fruition, having been choked out by the rocks of everyday life.

The third type of soil may be the most painful situation of all for the believer. The seed is cast upon thorns, where it takes root and sprouts. Before it can bear fruit, however, it is choked out by the thorns. Whereas in the rocky soil there is no root or firm understanding, in this soil there is a root, indicating a former receptivity of the heart. We are not told how much growth occurs before the plant is choked out by the worries of this life and/or the deceitfulness of wealth. How sad that in the end there is no fruit to account for it. The heart that was once receptive enough to produce growth now has become too preoccupied with the worries of the world to tend to the growth in order for it blossom. For the believer this is the enemy's greatest tactic. It would only make sense that the enemy would take drastic measures to prevent fruitfulness, especially to the tune of thirty-, sixty-, or one hundredfold. In our pursuit to be virtuous women, we must be realistic in our approach to the thorns. First, we must accept that where there is growth, thorns are not far away. Second, we must recognize them for what they are and remove them as they appear. If this is not done, it's only a matter of time before the thorns will choke out the plant, and growth will cease.

This is what the LORD says to the men of Judah
and to Jerusalem: "Break up your unplowed
ground and do not sow among thorns." (Jer. 4:3)

The fourth type of soil is the aim of every believer when it comes to receptivity to God's truths. This is the type of soil where godly legacies are made and spoken of for many years. What began, like the others, as a small sprout of growth, was tended to with careful attention. It is no longer a plant but a tree with fruit blossoming from a multitude of branches. The fruitful yield benefits not just the original plant but others as well. When we consider the pursuit to be a virtuous woman, virtue is too precious a commodity not to be shared. If tended to, it is sure to touch the lives of others as well.

You may have had times in your past when you heard a word from God, but because your heart was hard, you left God's message to you on the path for Satan to snatch away. Or perhaps you remember times when you initially got excited about a word from the Lord, but you didn't let it take root in your heart. If we are honest, most of us must plead guilty to other times when we allowed the thorns in our lives to choke out our passion for Christ.

I can think of several things we can do to improve our soil and make it more receptive to the seed of virtue. *First,* we need to be where the seed falls. Keep placing yourself under the teaching and preaching of the Word of God. *Second,* when a truth of God sets a flame in your heart, record it in a journal or in the margin of your Bible. *Third,* don't go it alone. Find a more mature believer and make yourself accountable. Have you noticed how we'll make a mental commitment to some action of discipleship, but the resolve dissolves if we don't tell somebody? We are much more likely to follow through if we have shared our commitment to change with someone else and have asked them to hold us accountable.

My heart has been all four types of ground at one time or another. Today it is the good soil, but that does not assure me that it will be tomorrow. I must do everything I can to keep my heart fertile and receptive to God's truth. To do that I need to maintain an active prayer life and stay in God's Word daily. Only then will I see the growth God intended.

Hearts represented by the good soil did not get there by accident but by the sovereign act of the Holy Spirit acting in cooperation with a person's desire and labor. By an act of their will, they labored long and hard to have this type of heart. We have no reason to assume that the good soil in the parable started out free from stones and thorns. Likewise, this type of heart is prepared, in spite of any hindrances, due to proper soil preparation. Someone picked out the stones. Someone hoed the weeds. Someone prepped the soil prior to planting time. Someone tended to the tender plants once they sprouted.

> *Sow for yourselves righteousness, reap the*
> *fruit of unfailing love, and break up your un-*
> *plowed ground; for it is time to seek the* LORD,
> *until he comes and showers righteousness on you.*
> (Hos. 10:12)

Only by seeking the Lord will we be able to break up the unplowed ground and soften our hearts to receive God's truth. His unfailing love will soften the hardest of hearts and leave us receptive to his teaching.

The truths I am writing about have changed my life. I want them to change yours too. Do you want to know what made the Proverbs 31 woman different? Are you willing to do what it takes to become this type of woman?

Simply put, a virtuous woman is a godly woman. Being a Christian does not ensure virtue. Proverbs 31 reminds us that virtuous women are a rare find. It is not a label that many will earn. As we explore the attributes of the Proverbs 31 woman in the following chapters, there will be some areas where you feel you are doing well and others that may need improvement. Regardless, do not grow discouraged. God does not expect perfection, but rather, perseverance.

Father, as you plant within our hearts the knowledge of what it is to be virtuous women, help us not only to be receptive to your teaching, but responsive, as well.

. . . for her price is far above rubies.
PROVERBS 31:10b (KJV)

What Are You Worth?

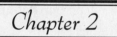

Chapter 2

I will never cease to be amazed at the drastic lengths to which God will go in order to draw a wayward heart unto himself. I remember vividly a large event I did for college women in Austin, Texas. The event began on a Friday night and concluded on Saturday afternoon. Ten minutes before the final closing session began, one of the volunteers came and shared how a foreign exchange student from Poland had stumbled into the church because she was lost and looking for directions to the University of Texas campus down the road. Several college women gave her the directions and then thought to invite her to stay for the remainder of the event. She agreed, and I was told that she was sitting up front on the second row. *Too bad!* I thought. *I gave my testimony last night; she should have been here then.* As I second-guessed the content of my closing message, I said a quick prayer for her and made my way onto the platform. My closing message was on the topic of worth. As someone who had misdefined my own worth for years, it was a subject close to my heart.

After giving the message and saying the closing prayer, I noticed that the foreign exchange student was sobbing, and several of the college girls were comforting her. Later that evening, I received a phone call from one of the girls. I was told that when the message ended, the student had broken down and between sobs in broken English said, "All my life I wonder where this worth come from—now, I know." The girls invited her to join them for dinner, and before the evening ended, they led her to faith in Christ. She had come to the event lost (literally), yet God made sure she left with the right directions—his direction.

Deep in the heart of every person is a desperate need to feel worth and value. Most people will end up defining their worth according to the world rather than by God's standard of measure. As women, we long to be told that we are worth more than the treasure of rubies. How we define our worth will impact every element of our lives. Defining our worth correctly is critical not only in our pursuit to be a virtuous woman but for our overall mental health. One can only wonder how many addictions, mental anxieties, and health problems could be avoided if the worth of the individual had been properly defined in the first place. The virtuous woman of Proverbs 31 had defined her worth according to God's standards.

How Do You Define Your Worth?

Stop and think about it for a minute. Make a mental list of the things that make you feel worthy and valued. Be honest. Now, ask yourself what would happen if everything on the list went away. Would you still feel worthy? The truth is, even the most mature of Christians will vacillate back and forth between the world's definition and

God's definition when it comes to worth. Are you not sure where you stand when it comes to properly defined worth? The four questions below will give you better insight.

1. Is your worth based on what others think or what God thinks?

> *Am I now trying to win the approval of men, or of God? Or am I trying to please men? If I were still trying to please men, I would not be a servant of Christ.* (Gal. 1:10)

I have always envied those who seem not to be influenced by what other people think. Of course there is a balance to this, and I am not referring to those who completely disregard the wishes of those around them. My envy quickly turns to anger if you cut me off on the freeway, allow your baby to cry during the movie I paid good money to see, show up thirty minutes late for a lunch appointment, or call my teenage son in the middle of the night. There is such a thing as common courtesy, and not to care what others think to the point where common courtesy is ignored is rude and selfish. I am talking about those who care less about what others think and more about what God thinks. As a chronic people-pleaser, I know firsthand the fallout that can occur from caring too much about what others think.

If we are honest, most of us would admit to having some people-pleasing tendencies. Deep down inside we want people to like us. Whether it's a forbidden morsel of gossip we trade or simply remaining silent when a conversation turns to religion, at our very core is a desire to fit in and not make waves. However, Scripture is clear that Christians are to be set apart from the world. In fact, we should probably be more concerned if we *are* fitting in. Romans 12:2 reminds us: "Do not conform any longer to the pattern of this world, but be transformed by the renewing of your mind. Then you will be able to test and approve what God's will is—his good, pleasing and perfect will." People-pleasers conform to the world around them. God-pleasers seek to please God.

When it comes to caring what others think, it is not just the world we worry about. If you've been a Christian for longer than a day, you may have noticed that not all Christians see eye to eye. I learned this the hard way early in my Christian walk. As a new mother, I had joined a Christian group for mothers with preschoolers. Overall, it was a wonderful experience, but there were times when the small-group discussion times sent me into a whirlwind of confusion and self-doubt. From subjects like breast-feeding versus bottle-feeding, homeschooling versus private schools versus public schools, and the age-old spank or not to spank debate, the opinions ran across the board. It was enough to drive any new mother crazy. As a new believer, I was easily influenced by opinionated women in the group (and trust me, every group has at least one!) who spoke up with authority and seemed to have a straight line to God when it came to determining his will for their lives—and everyone elses. I was not yet accustomed to filtering the opinions of others through God's Word and discussing them with God in my prayer time. As I matured in the faith, I realized that God, though presented with the same question, can give two different Christians two different answers.

In order to begin shedding our people-pleasing tendencies, it is critical that we understand the simple truth that no matter how hard we try, we will never be able to please everyone. If you haven't had to learn that one, just go into the ministry! Every person called into ministry should be required to take a "Surviving the Critics 101" course. I cannot tell you how many times I considered quitting ministry early on because of a criticism I received. My husband would gently remind me that I was not an independent contractor and that I needed to take it up with my Boss. Ideally, when we receive a criticism, we should weigh it against God's Word and objectively take it before God, asking him to show us if the criticism has any merit. As I have learned to do this, painful as it may be, there have been times when God confirmed that there was merit to the criticism. There have been other times, however, when after consulting the Lord, I have determined that the criticism was not valid.

Whoever stubbornly refuses to accept criticism
will suddenly be broken beyond repair.
(Prov. 29:1 NLT)

Though I have matured when it comes to dealing with the critics, I would be lying if I said it didn't get to me at times. I recall a large women's event years ago where I was speaker. For weeks after the event, I received numerous encouraging e-mails from women who had attended the event. Of course, I was quick to give God the credit for any good that had come from the event. And then it came: word got back to me (that's code for "someone told me") that I had offended a staff wife by wearing a pair of dress slacks on the platform when I spoke. Unbeknownst to me, this was a big no-no at the church. Mind you, my assistant had specifically asked for the dress code prior to the event and was told by someone on staff that dress slacks were acceptable. Had I known that was not the case, I would have been happy to abide by the rules.

Also on the lady's list of grievances was a comment implying that she thought I was an irresponsible parent. I had shared in one of my messages about a time when I had taken my high-school-aged son into an online chat room on a popular secular teen Web site. It was an open forum where teens could ask questions pertaining to spirituality. My purpose was to show my son how the majority of teens have embraced a philosophy that assumes that many paths lead to the same God. He was also able to converse with several teens. They asked him some tough questions, and it helped to sharpen his skills as he was put in a position where he gently had to defend the position that belief in Christ is the only path to God.

After the informant had finished with me, I hung up the phone, sobbed for a bit, and then called my husband with my well-rehearsed "I'm quitting" speech. My husband, being the godly man that he is, gently encouraged me to go directly to the Lord and seek his counsel in the matter. *Boom*, the pity party was over. After crying out to the Lord and consulting with a couple of godly women whom I consider to be my mentors, I determined that there was no validity to the criticism. It was hurtful all the same, but in the end I was able to shrug it off, knowing whom I aim to please.

We are not trying to please men but God, who
tests our hearts. You know we never used flattery,
nor did we put on a mask to cover up greed—
God is our witness. We were not looking for
praise from men, not from you or anyone else.
(1 Thess. 2:4b–6)

I get the feeling that the Proverbs 31 woman had come to the place in her life where she cared less about what others think and more about what God thinks. Her worth was not tied to the opinions of others.

2. Is your worth based on outward appearance or inner beauty?

> *Listen, O daughter, consider and give ear:*
> *Forget your people and your father's house. The*
> *king is enthralled by your beauty; honor him, for*
> *he is your lord.* (Ps. 45:10–11)

One study of Saturday morning toy commercials found that 50 percent of commercials aimed at girls spoke about physical attractiveness. The same study found that none of the commercials aimed at boys referred to appearance.[1] Another study found that women who spent just three minutes looking at fashion magazines felt depressed, guilty, and shameful.[2] Is it any wonder that women struggle with contentment when it comes to their appearance?

Have you made peace with the person God created you to be, or are you in the habit of comparing yourself to others? To not appreciate who we are is to imply that God could have done a better job when he knit us together in our mother's womb. Women who can claim with confidence that they are "fearfully and wonderfully made" in spite of that unsightly blemish, those ears that stick out, that bigger-than-average nose, or their heavyset frame are acknowledging that God knew what he was doing when he created them. The key to Psalm 139:14 comes at the end of the verse:

> *I praise you because I am fearfully and won-*
> *derfully made; your works are wonderful,*
> *I know that full well.* (Ps. 139:14)

Rare is the woman who can look in the mirror and confidently tell God, "Your works are wonderful!" The key is to "know that full well." It is especially difficult when we are bombarded constantly with images of waif-thin models who look as if they subsist on lettuce leaves and rice cakes. They may portray the culture's idea of the ideal woman, but it certainly isn't representative of the norm. The average woman is five-foot-four and 140 pounds and wears a size 14.[3] In fact, rare is the woman who matches the "ideal" hourglass figure presented by the majority of models. Not to mention that many of the models' pictures have benefited from airbrushing and computer enhancement. What is portrayed as ideal is, in actuality, unattainable for most women. It will be a constant source of frustration for anyone who thinks she is one diet shy of the perfect body.

There is no doubt that body image has a direct link to worth for most women. One study found that body satisfaction was highly associated with general self-esteem. Those who are satisfied with their bodies are more likely to have a higher self-esteem. This is not surprising considering how few women have made peace with the readout on the scale or their reflection in the mirror. For those who have, it brings a sense of accomplishment that would logically lend itself to a higher self-esteem. However, it gets out of balance if our worth is dependent on the measure of our esteem. Our esteem will fluctuate but our worth should not.

One would assume that as women get older and more mature, they would become more rational and accepting when it comes to their body image. This is not the case. A study found that women aged 20 to 29 and women aged 60 to 69 had almost the same degree of dissatisfaction with their bodies and wished they could be thinner. Women in the 40 to 59 age group were the most dissatisfied age demographic overall.[4] As someone who just recently entered the most dissatisfied age demographic, I can certainly understand the frustration of my sisters who are in the "fabulous forties and fifties" phase of life. I have never really struggled with my weight; however, as I approached 40, I began to notice that either my clothes were shrinking or I was growing. Not wanting to accept defeat, I continued to rationalize that if I could lose about five to ten pounds, I could get into my old clothes. Not that I don't like an excuse to shop, but buying new "bigger" clothes wasn't my kind of shopping. I settled the mental debate by buying a few pairs of pants in the next size up and a twelve-pack of Slimfast shakes. I refused to accept that with age my body shape had changed (therapists refer to this as "denial").

The Slimfast craze only lasted about a week, as I was never able to find a flavor that could satisfy my craving for Grande Vanilla Lattes at Starbucks. Unfortunately, the emotional battle went on for several years. I'm not sure when my attitude adjustment occurred, but one day while shopping, I pulled clothes from the rack in my actual size. Normally, when shopping for pants, I would subject myself to the standard dressing room torture where you try on clothes in your smaller size of past years, just to make sure you didn't miraculously shed weight by osmosis of wishful thinking. I finally reasoned that I was well within my required weight range and that it was unreasonable to expect that I would ever return to my old size. It was a first step in my efforts to make peace with my post-forty reflection in the mirror.

Why do so many women, myself included, torture themselves when it comes to body image by clinging to a perceived "ideal" of what we should look like? An ideal usually conceived in our early years—one that made no allowances for childbirth and the natural aging process. Why can't we accept that we are "fearfully and wonderfully made" no matter what our size or shape?

There is nothing wrong with wanting to look our best. The Bible tells us that are bodies are the temple of the Holy Spirit. As a result, we should show respect to his temple by keeping it properly maintained. When we redirect our focus from outer beauty to inner beauty, it certainly does not mean we disregard our appearance altogether. Proper grooming is just as much a part of maintaining the temple as eating right and exercising. There is a balance when it comes to how we look. If we focus too much on what we look like and it becomes more of a priority than the attention we give to developing qualities that would lend to inner beauty, it is out of balance. If we focus on developing qualities that lend to inner beauty yet have little regard for what we look like on the outside, it is out of balance.

> *Your beauty should not come from outward adornment, such as braided hair and the wearing of gold jewelry and fine clothes. Instead, it should be that of your inner self, the unfading beauty of a gentle and quiet spirit, which is of great worth in God's sight. (1 Pet. 3:3–4)*

3. Is your worth based on what you do or on what Christ did?

Another contributing factor to misdefined worth is a focus on performance. From the time we are young, we learn what will earn the world's applause. Whether it was a first-place ribbon in the science fair, a part in *The Nutcracker,* your name on the honor roll, or a spot on the cheerleading squad, everyone has at least one memory of a moment when time stood still and the ring of praise or, better yet, the thunder of applause echoed in our ears. Whatever it was, it probably gave a boost to our esteem and left us wanting more. Most of us, if we are honest, would admit to basing our worth, to some degree, on our performance and our accomplishments. To receive approval for something we have done can leave us feeling a sense of worth and validation. There is nothing wrong with cultivating our God-given gifts and talents and using them to the best of our abilities. In fact, in the parable of the talents (Matt. 25:14–30), God reminds us that we are to be good stewards with what we have been given. However, often this gets out of balance when worth is defined by accomplishments. For this person, to take away the accomplishments would leave them feeling worthless.

When we read about the Proverbs 31 woman, we need to beware. We could easily read our own performance-based worth into the chapter and think she had great worth because she did such great works. Not so. The Proverbs 31 woman had worth "far above rubies" because of who she was in God's eyes, not because of her noteworthy achievements.

Scripture is clear that "all our righteous acts are like filthy rags" (Isa. 64:6). Because of this, it is impossible to find favor with God based on works or good deeds. We are saved by grace and grace alone (Eph. 2:8–9). Our churches are filled with people who have hidden that verse in their hearts but nonetheless are still knocking themselves out to earn God or man's favor. I'm sure you've met this spiritual dynamo—she's the one who can organize the entire women's retreat, take a lead role in the church musical, and organize meals for the family who just had a baby, all to the amazement of others. At first glance she appears to have it all together, but rest assured, somebody is getting the dregs of this woman's life, and it's probably her family. How do I know? Because I've been this woman! Fueled by the approval and praises of others, if I wasn't performing, my sense of worth plummeted. While I was running off to help others, my poor family suffered.

My turning point came when the fallout from my misdefined worth exceeded the benefits of the temporary high I felt with each new accomplishment. As a child who had turned flips to earn the world's praises, I had grown into an adult who was doing the same thing. Even though I had tucked away the truth of Ephesians 2:8–9 in my heart, somewhere in the core of my being I doubted that God (and others) could love me just for me. I was drawn to the only measure for worth that I had ever known. Even today I find myself sometimes reverting back to performance-based worth, but then I stop, take a deep breath, and remind myself that God loves me for who I am, not what I do.

How about you? Is your worth based on who you are in Christ, or are you spinning a hundred different plates of good deeds to feel like you are worth something? A virtuous woman will get this in the right order. Ephesians 2:10 puts it into perspective: "For we are God's workmanship, created in Christ Jesus to do good works, which God prepared in advance for us to do." Our worth comes in knowing that we are his workmanship, and the "good works" result as a by-product of that truth.

4. Is your worth based on what you did in the past or on what Christ did to secure your future?

I'll never forget her face as she handed me a folded-up piece of paper. She could not speak. She came to the front in need of prayer at the end of a women's event. As I stood face-to-face with her, my heart broke. Her eyes were hollow and distant, as if she had given up long ago. Her face was stained with tears, and her hand was shaking uncontrollably as she handed me the slip of paper. Whatever was written on it obviously caused her too much shame to be able to speak it aloud as a prayer request.

I unfolded the paper and read, "God can never forgive me—I killed my unborn baby by doing crack cocaine." I looked up to find her staring at the ground, unable even to make eye contact with me. She had covered her face with her hands; her body was shivering as she silently sobbed. I wrapped my arms around this precious woman and said, "You've come to the right place. I have good news for you."

She had been a Christian for years, yet she had been unable to understand God's message of forgiveness. Somehow she had imagined it was possible to reach a point where her sin could outweigh God's ability to forgive. I don't know where she is today, but when she left that day, her face radiated with the freedom only Christ can give. She came lacking worth and left with her worth redefined. With God's help she was able to begin putting the past in its place.

As I have served in ministry, I have been overwhelmed at the number of hurting women I have met along the way who have allowed their pasts to impact the present. For many, the idea of being labeled a "virtuous" woman may seem impossible because of past not-so-virtuous choices. Did the virtuous woman of Proverbs 31 make virtuous choices at every crossroads in her life? We don't know her full story, but one thing is certain: a squeaky clean past is not a qualification when it comes to becoming a virtuous woman. If that were the case, I would not be writing this book.

A Woman with a Past

When I came to know Christ in my college years, I was loaded down with guilt and shame over a past that could be labeled anything but "virtuous." If someone had told me in those first several years that I would someday write a book with the word *virtuous* in the title, I would have said, "Yeah, right—is my name Pollyanna?" No wonder I ran from passages like Proverbs 31 during those years— I couldn't hold a candle to Little Miss Perfect. I wanted to read about someone in Scripture whom I could relate to, someone with a past who, in the end, made peace with her not-so-virtuous past. And then I found her one day when I was reading in the Gospel of John. A woman, a well, and a chance encounter with a Man who made her an offer she couldn't refuse. She came to the well with a past and left with a future. Her story offers hope to every woman who has ever felt "worthless" or ashamed over events in her past. More importantly, it offers a glimpse of how the Savior will respond to any woman who has yet to find relief for the ache that resides in her heart.

I don't know what your story is—maybe you don't have a much of a past and have managed consistently to make virtuous choices along the way. Let me encourage you to continue reading. This story may not be for you, but it is only a matter of time before you encounter a modern-day woman at the well. What will you say to her? What will you say to the woman who has had an abortion and cannot seem to forgive herself? Or the woman who has had an adulterous affair? Or the woman who can't seem to kick the addiction that enables her temporarily to dull her pain? The list goes on and on—masses of women lining up at the well and looking for something to set them free. Women who want with all their hearts to someday be remembered as virtuous women but who aren't sure if it's even possible. Yes, count me in as one of those women. As I read about the Samaritan woman on that particular day years ago, I could not only relate to her—I became her.

You probably remember the story. The drama unfolds with Jesus sitting at a simple well during the hottest part of the day. The disciples had gone into town to buy food, and Jesus rested, weary from the journey as they traveled from Judea to Galilee. How amazing that our Savior traveled like a simple commoner, unable to afford the luxury of traveling by horse or chariot. We are reminded of his humility and humanity as he sat at the well trying to catch his breath from the journey. Most likely his thoughts were consumed with the work yet to be done and the growing persecution of the Pharisees that had hastened his departure from Judea. Regardless, a divine appointment was on the books with a woman from Samaria. Unbeknownst to the woman who approached the well, her life was about to take a drastic turn. She came for the purpose of drawing water—or so she thought.

When Jesus asked the woman for a drink, she was clearly taken aback that he would even bother to speak to her. The Samaritans were of mixed blood and religion and were scorned by the Jews. The prejudices of the Jews against the Samaritans went back more than five hundred years; thus, they rarely communicated. Also, it was very unusual for men to speak to women in public—even to their own relatives. Another interesting fact is that water was available in the village of Sychar where the woman lived. Some theologians speculate that her trek out to the well was symbolic of the ostracism she experienced in her village over the sinful choices she had made. This woman had no servants to draw the water, so she traveled alone, carrying not only her watering pot but a weighty burden of guilt and shame. One can only imagine the thoughts that ran through her mind as she journeyed to the well. Like so many women today, she probably questioned how she had made such a mess of her life. Maybe she even rehearsed in her mind ways to break free from the sin that plagued her life.

Regardless of whether Jesus had planned all along for this divine appointment or her timely arrival just happened to put her in just the right place at just the right time is of little concern. Clearly, Jesus knew who she was the minute she approached the well. Mind you, there are no coincidences with God. When you stop and consider the fact that Jesus had a short three-year public ministry with much to accomplish, in addition to the fact that he was accustomed to drawing large crowds, then the thought that he took time out of his day to meet one-on-one with a woman living in sin is overwhelming. God incarnate felt that the meeting—to lift the burden of guilt from a foreign woman—was important enough to merit time from his short tenure on this earth. What then must his attitude be toward your sin and mine?

I find it interesting that Jesus began his conversation with the woman by asking her for a drink, yet he had nothing to draw the water. It makes you wonder if he was really thirsty or if the question was meant to quickly turn the conversation to living water. He went on to tell her that if she had living water she would not thirst again. Her curiosity was peaked, and she inquired about where she could get this water. Jesus then told her to "Go, call your husband and come back" (John 4:16). After responding that she had no husband, Jesus proceeded to tell her the details of her past and that she had had five husbands and was currently living with a man who was not her husband. Clearly shocked, she speculated that he was a prophet and said, "'I know that Messiah' (called Christ) 'is coming. When he comes, he will explain everything to us'" (John 4:25). Jesus then confessed his true identity, telling her, "I who speak to you am he" (John 4:26).

This begs the question of why Jesus would tell her to go and get her husband if he knew all along that she didn't have a husband. Doesn't it seem a bit cruel? This thought crossed my mind when I initially read the passage, but upon looking at it more closely, I see two reasons why he would bring up a topic that was a source of pain to the woman. First of all, he wanted her to understand that he was more than a mere man sitting at a well. Why would she trust the power of the "living water" if the one dispensing it was an average guy sitting at a well? Second, he told her to get her husband because it was necessary to first call attention to her sin. In doing so, he was able to make her aware of how desperately she needed living water.

He is the atoning sacrifice for our sins, and not only for ours but also for the sins of the whole world. (1 John 2:2)

It is no different today. When we come to know Christ, we must first acknowledge our sin and admit we need forgiveness. So often people imagine a wrathful, impatient God who deals harshly with disobedience. Jesus knew the Samaritan woman's past before she ever arrived at the well. He could have easily accused her up front and told her, "Look, lady, I know exactly who you are and what you have done. I have what you need, and if you want it, you better get your act together, and then I'll consider giving you this living water!" It sounds ridiculous, yet often Christians (and non-Christians) are hesitant to approach God because they think he would not welcome them until they have changed their sinful ways. Jesus modeled unconditional love to the woman at the well by offering her living water without making it contingent upon her changing her behavior first. It is a beautiful picture of a holy God bestowing his grace upon sinful man.

Charlotte Elliot, a modern-day woman at the well, responded to this same offer when a Swiss evangelist visited her home one afternoon in 1822. She was an invalid woman filled with despair, and he impressed upon her heart this truth: "You must come just as you are, a sinner, to the Lamb of God that taketh away the sin of the world." Miss Elliot heeded the man's advice and did just that. From that day forward, she recognized the day of her salvation each year as her spiritual birthday and celebrated it accordingly. The evangelist's words were not forgotten, and fourteen years after her conversion, she penned the words to this timeless hymn:[5]

> *Just as I am, without one plea,*
> *But that Thy blood was shed for me,*
> *And that Thou biddest me come to Thee—*
> *O Lamb of God, I come, I come!*

Just as I am, and waiting not
To rid my soul of one dark blot;
To Thee, whose blood can cleanse each spot,
O Lamb of God, I come, I come!
Just as I am, Thou wilt receive,
Wilt welcome, pardon, cleanse, relieve;
Because Thy promise I believe,
O Lamb of God, I come, I come!
Just as I am, Thy love unknown
Hath broken every barrier down;
Now, to be Thine, yes, Thine alone,
O Lamb of God, I come, I come!

How grateful I am that God was willing to accept me just as I am. I only wish that I had responded with the same initial enthusiasm that the Samaritan woman displayed. After conversing with Jesus, John 4:28 tells us that she forgot her water jar in her rush back to the village to tell the townspeople about her encounter with the Messiah. She was no longer interested in drawing water— not when she could partake of living water. As a result of her contagious enthusiasm, we are told that the people of Samaria made their way to see Jesus. Many of the Samaritans from that town believed in him because of the woman's testimony: "He told me everything I ever did" (John 4:39). The Samaritan woman had a lasting impact for generations to come because she recognized the power of living water and believed in the One who dispensed it.

Have You Left the Well?

The story certainly has a happy ending, but it could have gone much differently. Imagine the Samaritan woman responding to Jesus' offer of living water with,

"Thanks, but I just can't take it. My sin is far too great for your living water." As absurd as it sounds, many of us have done just that when it comes to God's forgiveness. We may still be hanging out at the well, burdened by the same shame and condemnation that brought us there in the first place. Some of us may have received living water yet failed to recognize the power it possesses. We stand there shuffling our feet in doubt, wondering how he could ever forgive us for some of the things we have done. Don't be fooled; God does not appreciate a woe-is-me attitude when it comes to sin. To doubt his forgiveness is to imply that the death of his Son was just not enough. It minimizes the power of the cross. When Christ died, he cried out, "It is finished." He did not footnote the statement with "unless you have had sex outside of marriage," "unless you have committed adultery," "unless you have blasphemed my name," "unless you have had an abortion." He simply said, "It is finished." Corrie ten Boom once said, "He casts our sins into the deepest ocean and then he places a sign out there that says 'no fishing allowed.'"[6] It may be time for you to acknowledge that "it is finished."

Like the Samaritan woman, we too have a choice when it comes to leaving the well. We too have the same potential to impact generations to come, but we must first turn our backs on the well and begin our journey away from the well.

On the last and greatest day of the Feast, Jesus stood and said in a loud voice, "If anyone is thirsty, let him come to me and drink. Whoever believes in me, as the Scripture has said, streams of living water will flow from within him."
(John 7:37–38)

If Jesus' offer of living water covers sin and shame, we must wonder why so many Christian women are still stuck at the well, unable to put the past in its place. Could it be the work of the enemy? Absolutely! Satan's greatest desire is to gain souls for an eternity. Once we come to know Christ, Satan loses the opportunity to have us for eternity. However, second-best would be to see Christians stuck at the well, doubting the power of living water. Think about it. If someone is failing to realize the power of the Holy Spirit, what would compel them to share that power with others? Satan would like nothing more than to render women ineffective as believers in Jesus Christ. We must recognize Satan for who he really is. Christian women who are burdened with shame and guilt are no worry to him. He knows that if they stay at the well in bondage to their pasts, they will have little impact when it comes to furthering the kingdom of God.

My people have committed two sins: They have
forsaken me, the spring of living water, and have
dug their own cisterns, broken cisterns that cannot
hold water. (Jer. 2:13)

Your pursuit to become a virtuous woman will be in vain if you fail to accept and appreciate God's forgiveness when it comes to your sin, whether it is in the past or the present. I used to think it would be a luxury to forget my past sins. However, I have come to the conclusion that the purpose of our remembering past sin is to remind us of what Christ has done for us. It should leave us feeling overwhelmed with gratitude rather than feeling shame and condemnation. Once the truth of the cross begins to take root in your heart, you will never be the same again.

Make a mental list of all your sins and failures, those things that bring you to your own well with Jesus. If you're really brave, write them down on a piece of paper. Now draw a cross over your list and write the banner "It is finished" over the top. Can you acknowledge that it is finished? If you struggle with guilt and condemnation over the past, meditate on the following Scriptures:

As far as the east is from the west, so far has he removed our transgressions from us. (Ps. 103:12)

Blessed are they whose transgressions are forgiven, whose sins are covered. Blessed is the man whose sin the Lord will never count against him. (Rom. 4:7–8)

Therefore, there is now no condemnation for those who are in Christ Jesus. (Rom. 8:1)

Their sins and lawless acts I will remember no more. (Heb. 10:17)

No sin is too great for the living water of Jesus Christ. To remain at the well is to further sin. What an insult to refuse our Lord's offer! Jesus took our sin to the cross in exchange for living water. He bore our sin and chose to die that we might live. When the magnitude of the cross sinks in, our worth will be redefined. If we have not been forever changed by the living water offered by Jesus Christ, we missed something at the well. Each of us has reason to visit the well. Each of us is in desperate need of living water. With one drink of living water, we take on a new identity. We become holy and blameless in God's sight. When he looks at us, he sees in us the righteousness of Jesus Christ. If that isn't a life-changing thought, I don't know what is. True worth is found at the well of forgiveness.

The Samaritan woman impacted Samaria for generations to come because she was faithful to take Jesus up on his offer of living water, consume (experience) living water, leave the well, and share living water with others. Will your faithfulness impact future generations in the same way?

ɷ ɷ ɷ

A virtuous woman will recognize that her worth has nothing to do with appearance, talent, or the opinions of others. She will recognize that her past belongs in the past and a future awaits her. A virtuous woman has worth far above rubies because she recognizes that her worth comes from who she is in Christ.

Come, all you who are thirsty, come to the waters. (Isa. 55:1a)

She selects wool and flax and works with eager hands.
She is like the merchant ships, bringing her food from
afar. She gets up while it is still dark; she provides food
for her family and portions for her servant girls.
She sees that her trading is profitable,
and her lamp does not go out at night.

PROVERBS 31:13–15, 18

No Time to Waste

Chapter 3

I have tried everything. In my attempt to be more efficient, I have purchased every organizational tool known to mankind—giant wall calendars, memo recorders, Day-Timers, and a Palm Pilot. When all else fails, I have even highlighted my hair for the blonde excuse. Each time I start off driven by a newfound commitment to bring order to my chaotic life, but days later I am back to my old ways. So, what constitutes my "old ways"? Scribbling notes, appointments, and reminders on whatever I can find at the moment—napkins, old receipts in my purse, chewing gum wrappers, checkbook stubs, an envelope from the junk-mail pile. I knew it was time for a new organizational system when I got angry at one my kids for using a napkin for its intended purpose and then throwing it away. The nerve of that child! It just so happened that the orthodontist appointment was scribbled on it. I shudder to think of how many hours I have spent tearing my house apart looking for priceless napkins, corners of envelopes, and tiny scraps of paper containing valuable information.

In this chapter we will discuss the Proverbs 31 woman's knack for efficiency. Call it a hunch, but I don't think she relied on the napkin method when it came to keeping her life in order. Suffice it to say that I feel highly unqualified to tackle the subject of efficiency. I tried to justify leaving it out of the book, but efficiency appears to be a major theme of about one-third of the Proverbs 31 passage. So with great conviction and a teachable heart, I have asked the Lord to show me his truth and, more importantly, to help me implement it in my life.

ev ev ev

Let's face it—the Proverbs 31 woman was no sluggard. Just reading the passage is enough to throw the average woman into guilt mode. However, it would be unwise to measure ourselves in a literal sense against her accomplishments. Times have changed, and many of the things the Proverbs 31 woman did in order to be efficient would actually be considered inefficient in today's culture. Try telling your fashion-conscious teenage daughter that you will be sewing all of her school clothes. That should go over *real* well. Of course, you can't start sewing until you have whipped up a batch of thread from the wool and flax you just happen to have lying around the house.

This woman was obviously busy and had much to accomplish on an average day. A coffee drinker, no doubt. She was probably doing espresso shots throughout the day. Did she ever rest? During the times in which she lived, inefficiency could be a matter of life and death if it resulted in an inability to acquire the basic necessities needed to survive.

A sluggard does not plow in season; so at harvest time he looks but finds nothing. (Prov. 20:4)

What would she be like today? Would she swear off every time-saving gadget on the market and insist on doing things the hard way? Would that be an efficient use of her time? There is certainly merit to many of the gadgets we have grown accustomed to that enable us to make the most of every minute.

My microwave recently went out, and for one week I had to resort to heating things up the old-fashioned way. I felt like a pioneer woman standing over the hot stove boiling water and cooking my frozen vegetables. When my new microwave finally arrived, it had a new feature that made all my suffering worth the wait. With one touch of the "quick start" button, it will heat whatever is in the microwave for thirty seconds. No more crampy fingers from having to press three buttons to heat my coffee! Now, *that's* efficient!

How did we ever live without our computers, microwaves, and cell phones? Remember back in the old days when we had to look things up in encyclopedias or go to the library to research a topic? Now, with the click of a mouse, we can "google" any word or topic and have thousands upon thousands of results within seconds. Just putting "Proverbs 31 woman" into the Google search engine yielded 134,000 online results! And to think that our kids have known no other way of life. I recently shared with my kids that telephone answering machines didn't come out until I was in college. I told them that I got used to the constant ringing of phones up and down the halls of my dorm at all hours of the day and night. There was no answering machine to pick up the calls and allow the callers to leave their messages. My kids stared at me in total disbelief, unable to imagine anything so horrible. Surely this beats our parents' lame "I walked two miles to school in the snow" story! My youngest, in deep thought, finally spoke and asked, "Mom, why didn't they just call you on your cell phone?"

Today I can't imagine life without an answering machine. In fact, I find it annoying if I call someone and they don't have one. Talk about inconvenient! I can't scratch it off my list because I have to keep trying until I reach them. And while we're on the subject of annoying, what about the folks who don't have call waiting? I have one rebel friend who refuses to pay extra for this convenience. Every time I call her and get a busy signal, I threaten to end the friendship when I finally do get through.

Perhaps most ironic is that in spite of all the time-saving gadgets on the market, we seem to have less time than ever. Maybe the Amish people had the right idea all along—no e-mails to return, no cell phones constantly ringing, no Starbucks on every corner. OK, that last one snapped me out of the "grass is always greener" mode. And so it brings us back to the question: If the Proverbs 31 woman were alive today, would she take advantage of time-saving devices in order to be more efficient? Would she grow her own fruits and vegetables and kill the fattened calf or occasionally succumb to the already-baked rotisserie chicken at the supermarket? Would she stick with snail mail or take advantage of e-mail? Would she go all the way down to the shipyard to sell her linen garments to the merchant ships or would she list them on eBay? Does being virtuous mean we have to give up all of our modern conveniences and do everything the hard way? I sure hope not, or count me out of contention for the title.

Efficient = A Balance Between Work and Play

The purpose of time-saving devices is to save time that could otherwise be spent doing things we enjoy. It would be easy to conclude after reading the Proverbs 31 passage that the virtuous woman had a rigid "all work and no play" philosophy and, therefore, would not condone such gadgets. My guess is that her "to do" list originated out of necessity and her lack of leisure time was not by choice. Some, upon the discovery that she "does not eat the bread of idleness" (Prov. 31:27), may conclude that relaxing was an unnecessary evil to be avoided. Before we give up coffee with friends, cancel the family vacation, or put down the novel we have been reading, we need to determine what constitutes *idleness*. Webster defines *idleness* as "uselessness; fruitlessness; laziness."

> *I went past the field of the sluggard, past the*
> *vineyard of the man who lacks judgment; thorns*
> *had come up everywhere, the ground was covered*
> *with weeds, and the stone wall was in ruins.*
> *I applied my heart to what I observed and learned*
> *a lesson from what I saw: A little sleep, a little*
> *slumber, a little folding of the hands to rest—and*
> *poverty will come on you like a bandit and*
> *scarcity like an armed man.* (Prov. 24:30–34)

Idle Time or Leisure Time?

In order to put this into proper perspective, I think we are safe to assume that the Proverbs 31 woman was not opposed to leisure time, but rather, useless or fruitless leisure time. Spending time with friends and family or relaxing after a hard day's work can hardly be considered useless or fruitless. In fact, one could argue that our hard work could become fruitless if we don't also *make* time to relax. The Proverbs 31 woman was opposed to idleness that served little or no purpose.

When Scripture speaks of "laziness," it is often contrasted with "diligence." There is a fine balance to leisure time. An "all play and no work" philosophy can lead to disastrous results. The fact that leisure time was in short supply in the Proverbs 31 woman's culture indicates that hard work was a way of life. For the most part they worked in order to survive. Today leisure time has become an expected commodity. It gets out of balance when it takes priority over accomplishing necessary tasks. Those of you with husbands who choose to spend the majority of their leisure time on the sofa watching the sports channel while the "honey do" list grows longer each day can yell out a hearty "Amen!" Let's also include our dear Christian sisters who are "golf widows." Leisure time should always come after our work has been accomplished or it becomes laziness.

If a man is lazy, the rafters sag; if his hands are idle, the house leaks. (Eccl. 10:18)

If we desire to emulate the Proverbs 31 woman's quality of efficiency, we must balance out our work and play. For some, this chapter may be a wake-up call that it's time to turn the TV off, put the book down, get off the

Internet, or quit doing whatever it is that distracts us from accomplishing the necessary chores in our day. Those things will still be there to enjoy when the work is done. For others, God may reveal that it's time to sit down, take a deep breath, and learn to relax. Maybe you have been going at breakneck speed and are running on empty. If you are a hard worker and the thought of relaxing makes you feel guilty, something is wrong.

Early on in my Christian walk, when I still tied my performance to my worth, I felt guilty at the thought of relaxing. I rationalized that if I wasn't doing something for the kingdom, it was wasted time. During this time, I remember going to a dear Christian friend's house to drop off something. She had been a Christian for quite some time, and I greatly admired her steady and consistent faith. I had assumed that her spiritual maturity came from a "no rest" philosophy, but I discovered otherwise when I arrived at her home. She invited me to stay for a minute and have coffee. Music was playing in the background and the sweet scent of fragranced candles permeated the air. As we sat down in her living room, I noticed her Bible on the end table as well as a novel of classic literature. I remember thinking to myself, *Is it permissible to read such things as fiction? Wouldn't God want us to only read our Bibles or Christian books?* Yet it was clear that my friend had her priorities in the right order.

I left her home that day knowing that God had used the experience to show me that rest was not only acceptable but necessary. It was a gentle reminder that he loves me not just for what I do but for who I am. Whether doing or being, he loves me just the same. Ladies, our God is a God of grace. He is not a rigid taskmaster who forbids us from resting. He modeled the importance of rest after hard work when he, himself rested on the seventh day of creation. Jesus also modeled the need to put work aside at times to fellowship with others or to be alone with the Father.

While laziness is one consequence of idle time, Paul warned the Thessalonians against another when he said, "We hear that some among you are idle. They are not busy; they are busybodies. Such people we command and urge in the Lord Jesus Christ to settle down and earn the bread they eat" (2 Thess. 3:11–12).

Ouch. No one wants to be thought of as a busybody. Our culture seems to think less of lazy, slothful behavior than meddlesome behavior. Both are equally detestable to God. Webster defines *busybody* as "one who officiously concerns himself with the affairs of others; a meddling person." Unwanted or uninvited advice is never pleasant, and truth be told, it rarely yields the intended results. We can all think of people who honestly feel it is their duty to fix everyone's lives for the presumed better.

It's hard to imagine the Proverbs 31 woman chatting with her best girlfriend about how so-and-so and her spouse are living well beyond their means, having purchased a new chariot with leather interior. It's hard to imagine her berating her sister for weaning her child too early from breast-feeding. She didn't have time for such silly matters. Perhaps the Proverbs 31 woman abhorred idleness because she feared the consequences it might produce in her own life, or maybe she had witnessed first-hand the damage it had produced in the lives of others.

If we are honest, we would all have to admit to times when we have been a busybody. If we have time on our hands, the devil will be faithful in trying to get us to fill it with things that are useless and unproductive. While time spent in fellowship with our girlfriends is not useless idle time (given it does not take priority over work we need to accomplish), if in that time we gossip or discuss matters that are of no concern to us, then it becomes misspent idle time. In conclusion, idle time is not wrong, but useless idle time is. Part of being efficient will be learning the balance between being a hard worker and spending our leisure time wisely.

Efficient = Organized

Few would argue that organization lends itself to efficiency. Years ago, before I had formally entered a speaking ministry, I was asked to fill in on a panel for someone who had to cancel at the last minute. It was for a group of mothers of preschoolers, and the topic of discussion was "organization." I tried everything to get out of it. I told the woman who called to ask (beg?) me to fill in on the panel about my napkin method of organization to dissuade her, but she still persisted. Clearly, this woman was desperate. Finally, I relented and agreed to sit on the panel under one condition: I would represent the messy contingency in order to bring a balance to the otherwise lopsided panel of organization gurus. To have sat on the panel as an authority on organization would have ventured on being hypocritical.

The next day the panel members were introduced one at a time. Each one shared briefly what their area of expertise was regarding organization. The first woman shared that she would address coupon clipping and developing a filing system for your recipes. The next woman shared that she would address organizing your pantry and making your own gift wrap. Then it was my turn. I was feeling a bit overwhelmed at the discovery that Martha Stewart had been cloned twice over, and now I was serving on the same panel as her minions. While the women in the audience waited patiently to hear what my area of expertise was regarding organization, I decided that honesty was the best policy. I took a deep breath and asked the women in the audience to raise their hands if they're into gift bags, write their "to do" list on napkins, or rifled through a giant pile of clothes to find what they were currently wearing. Based on the response of the audience, I discovered that I was not alone in my lack of organization. In fact, a woman approached me at the end and asked me to be on her weekly radio program to discuss organization from a "wannabe" perspective!

That was many years ago, and while I have improved some when it comes to being more organized, I still have a long way to go. As I have matured in the faith, I have also come to realize that organization, while it can be a learned trait, is mainly influenced by personality or temperament. Some people will have a high need for things to be organized and orderly, while others will not. My theory was proven one day when my daughter and I set out in search of a trunk for summer camp. We didn't have much time, so I went to a store that specializes in containers of all shapes and sizes. It is every type-A person's dream come true. They have containers for every item in your pantry. They have containers for every item in your garage. They have containers for every item in your closet. It is ridiculous; I think they even have containers for containers. My daughter, who is a real neatnik, had never been in the store before. When we walked through the doors, surrounded on all sides by row after row of containers, she stopped and grabbed her heart and gasped. "I must be in heaven," she said. "This is what heaven looks like." Funny, I was thinking just the opposite. I broke out in cold sweats the minute I walked through the doors.

Try as I may, I will never be *that* organized. I don't want to be that organized. If someone else wants to be that organized, great—it's just not me. Trust me, I've tried, and it doesn't work. I like a tidy house, but I don't spend hours and hours keeping it clean. If people stop by and it's not picked up, no big deal. I want a home, not a showplace. If they judge me by my house, they're not the type I want for friends anyway. There is such a thing as going overboard when it comes to organization. Some people are organized to a fault and end up spending more time maintaining their system of organization than the time they were hoping to save by being organized. Being overly organized does not always lead to efficiency. Just as it is important to balance work and leisure, it will also be important to balance organization.

When it comes to organization, my husband and I are the perfect example of both extremes. I knew I was in big trouble when after one of our wedding showers he pulled the instruction manuals out of each appliance and highlighted the main points. He thought he was helping by highlighting them in order to save me the time of reading them in their entirety. Little did he know, I had never looked at an instruction manual in my life. I lived by the philosophy that if the appliance couldn't be figured out just by turning it on, it wasn't worth having. If there's a problem on down the road, *then* you look at the manual (if you can find it). Whether we are deciding on a vacation destination, a new appliance, or a health club membership, he devotes great thought and research to it before making a decision. No doubt, he has saved us much heartache, money, time spent in repairs, etc., by doing research on the front end. Sometimes, he gets a little carried away, and I have had to tell him, lovingly, to lighten up.

Even though I give him a hard time, I must admit that most of the time his research comes in handy. When we planned a trip to Disney World (did I say "we"?), I teased him mercilessly about all the time he put into the trip. He must have gone through an entire print cartridge and a ream of paper in the process of gathering facts in his online research. He even read an entire book devoted solely to Disney World! By the time he was done, he had the entire trip planned from start to finish. There was not a single millisecond unaccounted for in the itinerary.

The first morning we were to head to the park, he was like a drill sergeant, rushing us out the door of our hotel room to beat the crowd for the free continental breakfast downstairs. After breakfast, we headed for the park. We laugh about the memory to this day because he made me get my coffee in a "to go" cup, and all they had was a soup container. I ended up spilling it down the front of my white shirt while attempting to drink the coffee from the Styrofoam trough while hustling to the park to beat the crowd.

When we arrived at the entrance of the park, it was not yet opened. This was, of course, part of the plan. When the gates finally opened, I thought I was going to lose it when he barked, "Quick! Head past the crowd to the #47 ticket line! The book says it's always the shortest!" We hustled past everyone and, sure enough, we were first in line. While in line, he began to detail the plan of attack (according to his trusty book) for riding the rides.

He knew exactly which rides to avoid in the morning and where to go to escape the crowd. When the gates opened, everyone seemed to bolt in the direction of the most popular rides (as predicted by the book and backed up with research). We headed in the opposite direction with a handful of other people, all of whom had probably read the same book. Sure enough, we were first in line to the rides. We rode some of the rides over and over again. He knew where the Disney characters' dressing rooms were and when they were due to come out and make their way to the long line of people waiting for autographs. The book said they would sign autographs en route to the big crowd of people if you were able to catch them at their dressing rooms. Sure enough, we got autographs, pictures, and hugs, and zoomed past the long line of people on our way to the next ride. When it was time for lunch, he knew which restaurants were the least crowded. It was amazing! (I joked at one point when taking my daughter to the bathroom and asked him which stall we were supposed to use.) His research paid off, and it was not only an efficient use of our time but a great memory. Now I hesitate before teasing him—unless, of course, he starts highlighting instruction manuals again!

I am more of a stimulus-response, live-for-the-moment kind of gal. Bless his heart, he probably didn't know what he was signing up for when he married me. However, over the years we have come to appreciate the strengths of each other's temperament when it comes to organization. He has learned that not everything has to be researched and that it's OK to be spontaneous at times. On the other hand, I have gained a greater appreciation for doing research on the front end in order to save time in the future.

I wonder if organization came easily for the Proverbs 31 woman. Did she have a junk drawer in each room? Did she occasionally discover food in her refrigerator that had been there so long that it had morphed into something that looked like it could walk away any minute? Did she have enough paraphernalia in the floorboard of her car to assemble a rocket ship, if necessary? My hunch tells me that the Proverbs 31 woman had found the balance when it came to being organized.

Efficient = A Good Steward

I love to shop, but I also love a good bargain. Rarely do I buy anything that is not on sale. My husband, on the other hand, hates to shop and will rarely buy anything, period. He's the type who will ask for needs for birthday and Christmas. On top of that, we have two different perspectives on what constitutes "needs." This is a guy who, when we were engaged, suggested that we blow off registering for china and ask for the equivalent in paper plates. I remember our first Christmas together after we were married. We had a simple Charlie Brown tree and a few token ornaments. The day after Christmas I took advantage of the sales and bought ornaments, tinsel, wrapping paper, and other Christmas *necessities*. I came home with my bargains, gloating to my husband that I had saved him 75 percent. He calmly replied, "If you had stayed home, you would have saved me 100 percent."

We have since learned to meet in the middle, which is code for "I got to keep the Christmas loot and my tree looked stunning the next year." My husband is not an ogre, and his hesitation to spend comes from a sincere effort to be a good steward with that with which we have been blessed.

One parable that illustrates the importance of being a good steward is the parable of the talents in Matthew 25:14–29. A master entrusted his property to his servants and gave one servant five talents, another servant two talents, and another servant one talent. The first two servants invested the talents given to them and doubled their master's money. The last one buried his talent and yielded nothing above the original talent. When they reported back to their master, the first two were commended for a job well done, while the last one was chastised for being a "wicked, lazy servant" (v. 26). The master then took his one talent and gave it to the servant with ten talents. The parable relates not only to the money God has entrusted to us but to our gifts and talents as well. It might seem "safe" and logical to bury what we have in order to safeguard it, but God expects us to utilize and expand that which he has entrusted to us.

The parable makes the point that it is equally as abominable to God to hoard our money or talents as it is to waste them in meaningless ways. Part of being efficient is learning to resist the urge to hang on to something that doesn't belong to us in the first place, while also being careful not to invest what he has given us into things that bear little or no fruit in the end.

Efficient = Learning to Delegate

Years ago I was having lunch with a godly woman whom I greatly admire, and we had a conversation that left me somewhat confused. I mentioned to her that I was working part-time from home and that in order to ensure that my family did not suffer as a result of my time spent working, I had hired a housekeeper to come in once a week. The hours spent cleaning my house could then be redirected to time spent with my family. I was shocked when she responded that part of "watch[ing] over the affairs of [my] household" (Prov. 31:27) was to keep my home in order for my family. I believe that was exactly what I was doing. I had my husband's full blessing and support. My salary more than covered the cost, and we were both at peace with the decision. What's more, anyone who has had a housekeeper knows that the house doesn't stay clean and tidy the whole week until the housekeeper returns. I still had clothes to wash, grocery shopping to do, meals to prepare, and much more. The housekeeper took care of the intense cleaning, and the hours I saved were spent ministering to my family in other ways. It was a win/win for everyone involved. I had no doubt that my decision left me more efficient overall.

Years later I ran across Proverbs 31:15 about the virtuous woman providing "portions for her servant girls." This woman wasn't exactly zipping off to play tennis at the country club while the hired help cleaned the house, did the laundry, and washed the baseboards. We are told that even *with* the help she still "gets up while it is still dark . . . and her lamp does not go out at night." And look who was left to prepare the food! If she was that busy with servant girls, what would her life have been like without them? The Proverbs 31 woman knew the value of delegating work to others so as to maximize her time and fulfill the task.

For some, delegation does not come easily. If you often find yourself mumbling, "It's just easier if I do it myself," you may need to ask yourself what is so easy about saving all the work for yourself, especially if others are willing to help. Perhaps what you are really saying is, "I like it better when it's done my way and my way alone." If your schedule is packed and you often find yourself feeling frustrated that you never seem to have enough time to get things done, is it really efficient to remake the kid's beds in the morning? Is it efficient to plan every detail of the church women's retreat when you have a committee of women who have signed up to help? Sure, there is risk involved if you delegate. You may not be able to pop a quarter on the bed covers, and the women's retreat may have a few kinks in it, but in the scheme of life, what's the big deal?

I realize that there are some situations when it would take more time to adequately train someone else than to do it ourselves. If time is a factor, then obviously it is best to do it ourselves. We can all think of times when we've knocked ourselves out to get a job done and grumbled and complained the whole way through. Part of learning to be more efficient will be learning to recognize times when it is conducive to spread the job out and delegate to others.

Efficient = Learning to Say NO!

When we learned to talk, one of our first words was most likely *no*! Regardless of all the practice we had saying this word in our early years, it seems to be one of the most difficult words for women to say in their adult years. Part of being efficient will be learning to say no to things that would otherwise leave us overcommitted, weary, and bitter. While I have been forced to learn to say no in order to juggle ministry and family, I still have a long way to go.

With book deadlines, speaking engagements, overseeing a national ministry, and most importantly, my obligations to family, my schedule is tight. I am famous for thinking on the front end that I can do it all. I do not want my family to get the dregs of my life because I have overcommitted myself to other things. I am a firm believer that those called to ministry as a vocation who also have families should view their families as their first ministry before attempting to serve others. However, this is easier said than done, and there have been times when my writing and speaking commitments have taken a toll on my family. In order to keep this from getting out of hand in the future, my husband and I came up with a system for accepting out-of-town speaking engagements: try to avoid two weekends in a row, limit the number of three+ day events, protect certain months, set aside time for writing, etc. It is not foolproof, but it has drastically improved. My office manager handles my calendar, and once it is full, she holds me accountable to the system. I have learned the hard way that once the calendar is full, saying yes to another invitation is saying no to family. In the process of writing this chapter, I even had to say no to my own church for an out-of-town women's retreat. As much as I wanted to do it, I knew that my family would pay the price.

How I wish I had learned to say no sooner! I think back on the years when my kids were young and I said yes to far too many things—homeroom mom, serving on the church council, leading Bible studies, teaching Sunday school, and the list goes on. All were worthy endeavors, but when combined, it was enough to justify putting me in a straitjacket and having me committed. What was I thinking?!

I remember a year when I organized the women's retreat at my church with my dearest friend, who also happens to be our pastor's wife. I should have seen a red flag when the first meeting was weeks after I had given birth to my second child. And this was not your average child. She was what my pediatrician referred to as a "high need" infant. That is a fancy label for a baby who cries nonstop when she's not being held and wants to breast-feed every two hours for a few minutes at a time. Yet full steam ahead on the women's retreat! I rationalized, "If not me, then who?" My friend Carolyn couldn't take over because she had also had her second child a couple of months before me. By the time the retreat rolled around, I was weary, grumpy, and running on fumes.

Carolyn and I are finally able to laugh about it now, but it was so ridiculous that our husbands had to stay in a pop-up camper on the retreat grounds with our tod-dlers and newborns because Carolyn and I were still nurs-ing our babies! Our sweet husbands are able to also laugh about it now, but they sure weren't doing a whole lot of laughing then. As I look back, I realize that my inability to say no was because I was still caught up in the perform-ance trap. Sadly, my family suffered while I was out trying to prove myself to whom? Others? God?

While we're on the subject of saying no, it is also nec-essary to learn to cut out extra unnecessary steps that in the end will most likely go unnoticed. Actually, this is one time when no comes pretty easy for me. Case in point: If you're short on time, why iron your preschooler's clothes if they are going to be wrinkled within the hour when he decides to roll down the hill at the park? For that matter, why iron your teenager's clothes before school when they are fully capable of ironing them themselves? Why make the crust for your pie from scratch when you can get the dough or pie shell at the supermarket? If you're short on time, why knock yourself out making a pot roast—sounds like "taco night" to me. If you're short on time, why agree to have the Sunday school fellowship at your house? What? You committed a month ago and had no idea you would be so swamped? Call a couple of people in the class, explain your dilemma, and ask them to host the party. Can't get out of it and you don't have time to clean the whole house? Whoop-de-do—close off all the upstairs rooms and tell everyone they are off limits. Don't have time to get the fresh flowers for the centerpiece? Let little Johnny pick wildflowers from the front yard you didn't have time to mow and put them in a pretty vase. I know this is a humbling thought, but the truth is, most people don't notice the extra steps you are taking anyway! If we are to be efficient, we must learn to be reasonable and cut out unnecessary steps.

I know this has been a convicting chapter for many women. I have been personally convicted just from writing it—maybe it was the fact that *every* night was "taco night" until I could get it finished. Remember, I am not an authority when it comes to the virtuous woman, and I am a fellow sojourner with you in the journey. If you, like me, have a long way to go when it comes to being efficient, ask God to help you, and take it one step at a time. Praise God, we serve a patient God who loves us no matter what. With that encouraging thought, I will close. Besides, I need to get to the store . . . we're out of taco shells.

*She considers a field and buys it; out of her
earnings she plants a vineyard. She sets
about her work vigorously; her arms are
strong for her tasks.*

PROVERBS 31:16–17

Wimps Need Not Apply

Chapter 4

I must confess that when it comes to the virtuous woman of Proverbs 31, I am guilty of stereotyping. In my mind I picture a June-Cleaver-like woman with a pleasant and soft-spoken voice. True to form, she is dressed in her Sunday best and pearls as she flits about the kitchen dividing her time between stirring her home-made concoction and setting the table with her fine china. Her reward comes when the family gathers around the table and she hears that familiar chorus of "Great pot roast, Mom!" She is quiet and humble, uncomfortable with the praises.

My stereotype weakened after reading that she considered a field and bought it, not to mention, with her own earnings. Would June Cleaver do that? Certainly not! Can't you just see her asking Ward to cosign the papers as he sits in his easy chair reading his newspaper? Then I read the next verse about planting a vineyard. Again, I struggled to

~ *69*

picture my June Cleaver prototype with sweat on her brow and dirt under her fingernails after a day spent planting a vineyard. This was no casual gardener. Words like *independent* and *confident* come to mind, which contrast with my previous stand-behind-your-man subservient stereotype. The June Cleaver stereotype I had imagined might bring home some of the bacon by selling Tupperware, but it fell apart when I tried to picture her cutting a land deal with her realtor, sans Ward. The verses extolling her independent and confident nature almost seem out of place with the rest of the passage.

Often when the passage is addressed, you hear no explanation for the verses pertaining to her land deal. If they are addressed, they are oftentimes treated as insignificant. I am certainly not trying to stir up controversy by addressing the meaning behind the verses, but I think we would all be wise to shed any previous stereotypes of the virtuous woman of Proverbs 31 being a doormat of sorts, incapable of independent thought. We can assume it's a given that she had her husband's blessing on the land deal or it would have contradicted previous verses in the passage. In fact, it illustrates the trust her husband had placed in her (Prov. 31:11), a trust, no doubt, that was well earned over the years. However, it seems to contradict the image many get of the submissive wife who dares not to make a move without her husband's permission.

The Proverbs 31 woman lived in a time period, mind you, that was generally oppressive to women, and it was certainly out of the norm for a woman to be using her earnings to conduct a real estate transaction. When the passage is taken in context as a whole, this woman was probably more similar to the rugged pioneer women of days past. She may have had maidens, but don't be fooled, they didn't handle the dirty work while she played a few rounds of tennis at the club. There was plenty of hard work to go around for everybody. Let's face it—she (and her maidens) would make the average contestant on the "Survivor" show look like a wimp.

There is no arguing the fact that the virtuous woman was a strong woman physically, mentally, and spiritually. Proverbs 31:17 implies a physical strength that was necessary to accomplish her daily tasks. Nonetheless, her strength did not diminish her femininity. The confidence she demonstrated in Proverbs 31:16 reminds us that she possessed the ability to earn an income, think for herself, and see a plan through to its completion. She showed independence, but it did not compromise her role as a submissive wife. Yet her greatest strength was undeniably in her God. Her strong, unyielding faith provided her with wisdom, confidence, and the ability to laugh at the days to come.

With this knowledge of the virtuous woman, my June Cleaver stereotype began to crumble. June Cleaver did not appear to be physically strong. The only time I could recall her strengthening her arms was when she was stirring a pot on the stove. Granted, let's give the woman credit—she lived a rather simple and trouble-free life. I can't picture her orchestrating a major land deal or, for that matter, any kind of deal that would require her to exercise some free-thought. For heaven's sakes, she leaned on poor Ward for *everything!* The house could be burning down around them, and she would have asked in that pleasant, docile voice, "Oh Ward, should we wake the boys?" As for spiritual strength, it was, at best, shallow in nature. I don't recall her sitting and reading her Bible or applying Scripture to the rearing of her boys. Why then have so many Christians come to interpret the Proverbs 31 passage as a call for women to be "domestic" rather than a call for them to be "strong?" In truth, the Proverbs 31 woman's domestic abilities were only one aspect that lent to her virtuous status. At the very core of virtue is strength.

Virtuous Empowerment

We live in a culture where strong women are esteemed. Unfortunately, it's not exactly the same brand of strength that defines virtue. In fact, it is quite the contrary. Our culture peddles a brand of strength to women called "empowerment" or, in its juvenile form, "girl power." This type of strength is equated to dominance and power, whether it is manifested in the workforce, relationships, or life in general. If you trace the concept of empowerment back to a point of origination, you would most likely end up at the crossroads of the radical women's liberation movement and the sexual revolution, both of which found their wings in the late 1960s and early 1970s. It is important to note that the concept of biblical virtue was a mainstay in culture prior to the onset of these two radical movements.

Today *virtue* is a scarcely used word thought by many to be an outdated concept of days past. Why opt for virtue when you can have *empowerment?* To possess virtue, you must strive for moral excellence, which in turn holds you accountable to a standard of right and wrong. Empowerment, on the other hand, is most often connected to the word *self,* which more adequately reveals its true mission—self-empowerment. It's all about ME! Self rules! With empowerment, anything goes because you have the power to choose your own standard of morality.

Seems I recall our dear sister Eve buying into the lie of empowerment. With one bite of the forbidden fruit, the serpent said her eyes would be opened, and opened they were—to a new concept called "good and evil." With this new knowledge she hoped to gain power, yet in the end she was left powerless. She was snared by what has become Satan's oldest trick in the book: the focus on self. The enemy knows what many of us have had to learn the hard way: *when the focus is on self, it is off God.* Women today are no different. Empowerment sounds so alluring. It promises to fulfill our innermost needs. In its most radical form it sends damaging messages to women of all ages. If you desire to climb to the top of the career ladder, yet it would require you to sacrifice your family on the altar of success, big deal! It's all about *you!* Why wait to have sex until you're married? Empowerment has no rules except "If it feels good do it," or "Look out for No. 1, and run roughshod over anyone who tries to get in your way."

Our young girls have been thoroughly indoctrinated into the pre-empowerment "girl power" movement. It is peddled to girls through fashion magazines, television, movies, music, and advertisements. The movement encourages them to be the aggressors in relationships; to pursue success at any cost; to dress any way they please, regardless if it is offensive; and to have sex with whomever they want whenever they want, with no strings attached. Sex has become recreational, having been downgraded from sacred to secular. They are taught to trample over anyone who might hinder them from worshipping almighty self. Whereas virtue encourages the pursuit of moral excellence, empowerment seeks to dominate and conquer. It is harsh, abrasive, and altogether unattractive. It is strength misused for purposes that are null and void of any meaning. Let's face it—it's Eve in the garden hungering for power only to be left hungry in the end.

We are several decades past the radical women's liberation movement and the sexual revolution, and the "progress" it was meant to bring for women has been overshadowed by broken marriages and families, an increase in addictions of every sort, an increase in depression among women, and an overall wake of whining, bitter, impossible-to-please women. And that, my sisters, is where we come in. We have the answer. We know the One who truly liberates. Jesus Christ liberated women some two thousand years ago when he cried out on the cross, "It is finished." True strength comes in knowing Jesus Christ. He is the source of strength for the virtuous woman. He is the only one who can satisfy a restless heart.

Virtuous Reality

I am not one to remain silent about the negative influences of the culture that compromise virtue. In fact, I am an activist to the core. My husband kids me about my activist nature and once said, "Thank the Lord you found the right cause." Amen to that! I could have easily been the girl who climbed up into a redwood tree in California and lived there for two years. She was willing to do whatever it took to protect the tree from the peril of a chainsaw in the hands of ambitious developers. While her devotion to the cause is admirable, I find it a shame that she was misguided in her allegiance to the created rather than the Creator. If she ever gets it straight, we could sure use her in the harvest!

My concern over the absence of virtue in our nation has framed my call to ministry. In 1998, Virtuous Reality

Ministries was born in the kitchen of my home. It began as an event ministry to college women with the purpose of encouraging them to make virtue a reality in their lives. It was met with an overwhelming response, yet I was concerned that the events seemed to be more of a recovery effort. Sadly, many college women (most were Christians) had already succumbed to the culture's influences and were reaping the consequences. While the effort to reach them with the message of virtue was a worthy one, I also began to pray that God would allow me to take the message to an even younger audience in the hope that it would be more of a preventative effort than a recovery effort. Several years later the ministry expanded to include an online magazine (www.virtuous reality.com) for middle school and high school girls, college women, and women. The purpose was to provide girls and young women with a wholesome alternative to the trashy virtueless fashion magazines.

Today, Virtuous Reality Ministries holds events across the country for girls in third to sixth grades and their mothers, middle and high school girls and their mothers, and college women. We even have a Web site where girls can sign a pledge of virtue that includes a commitment to moral excellence, strength, worth, and purity (including modesty). Girls from all over the world have visited www.virtuepledge.com and have made a covenant with God pledging themselves to biblical virtue. Studies have shown that pledges to purity yield positive results. To keep the pledge fresh in their minds, we send the girls a friendly reminder of their pledge to virtue every six months. What began in my kitchen with one volunteer has today expanded to an office with a growing staff. Whether through events, the Web site, or resources, the purpose is the same—expose the lies of the culture and encourage girls and young women to make virtue a reality in their lives.

I count it a tremendous privilege that God would consider using me in any capacity to proclaim his truths. It is mind-boggling to me that he would take someone like myself, who has experienced a not-so-virtuous past, and allow me to encourage others in the pursuit of virtue. I have experienced firsthand the consequences that come as a result of believing the lies of the culture. I followed the world's formula for becoming an ideal woman. It left me bitter, confused, and empty. In my emptiness, I cried out to God in my college years. God heard my cry for help, and my life has never been the same since. Now I am passionate about telling girls and young women that the world's formula for becoming an ideal woman is a *virtual reality*. True fulfillment comes in knowing that with God's help anyone can become a *virtuous reality*.

Virtuous Responsibility

President John Adams once said, "From all that I had read of history and government of human life and manners, I had drawn this conclusion, that the manners of women are the most infallible barometer to ascertain the degree of morality and virtue of a nation."

What would John Adams say if he were here today? Certainly he would be concerned about the manners of women, or for that matter, the lack thereof. While I don't think we can blame women entirely for the current state of our immoral culture, I believe there is a link between the radical women's lib movement stemming from the sexual revolution several decades ago and the moral freefall our culture is experiencing.

As hopeless as it seems at times, we must remember that we have been given the strength to counteract the negative influences of the culture. We must claim virtue not only for ourselves but also for our nation. It may seem like a losing battle to many, but be reminded—Christians are the majority in this country. We have been silent for far too long. Many of us have been bullied into silence as the culture preaches tolerance for anything but Christianity. I believe many Christian women have been hesitant to speak up because they have not felt it was part of their duty as a virtuous woman. I believe there is no greater force to change culture than a mass of angry Christian women who stand up and say, "Enough!" There is too much on the line not to speak up.

One Bible commentary defined *virtue* as "moral courage."[1] In our silence we have allowed our culture to be framed by moral relativism. Moral relativism is the pervasive thought of the day that basically says, "What's right for you may not be right for me, and vice versa." It is a system where each individual defines his or her own morality according to personal preference. Of course, we will not see a rebirth of virtue in this country unless we become more vocal in stating that there is one absolute standard of morality, as defined by God in his Word. This is not a politically correct viewpoint, so many Christians are hesitant to broach this topic with others. We must get past our fear of making others uncomfortable. There is a way to say, "That is wrong," and not be offensive.

It dawned on me not long ago that many people who embrace moral relativism and choose to live immoral lifestyles have not hesitated to shove their immorality in our faces. Some are militant about indoctrinating our youth into moral relativism with their battle cry of tolerance. As Christians, we have had to endure scantily clad pop stars who look like strippers, female pop stars kissing on national television, hip-hop lyrics that are degrading to women, television shows that glamorize homosexuality, uninvited porn in our e-mail inboxes, clothing stores using sex to sell to teens, and the list goes on and on and on. Why can't we be militant in return when standing for virtue? Our greatest weapon is our voice. We can cast a vote against the influences of the culture by letting our voices be heard. I've heard it said that evangelical Christians can determine a presidential election if the majority would just show up at the polls and vote.

One tangible way to take a stand for virtue is to vote for candidates who embrace moral viewpoints. Another way to stand for virtue is by e-mailing or calling companies who play a part in contributing to the moral depravity in our country. If necessary, we can even boycott companies who blatantly disregard virtue. I am proud to say that I have never purchased a single article of clothing from Abercrombie & Fitch. I refuse to contribute a single cent to a company that introduces a line of thong underwear to seven-to-fourteen-year-old little girls and shrugs it off as "cute" in a statement to the public. They had already crossed the line of decency long before with their quarterly porn catalogs featuring nude models and "advice" about masturbation, group sex, and sexual promiscuity. They have enraged M.A.D.D. (Mothers Against Drunk Drivers) by including a free tear-off spinner in their catalog to aid teens in drinking games. Many of these dear mothers have lost children to drunk drivers, yet the company shrugged off their complaints. I realize that we must choose our battles, and this is one that many Christians have chosen not to fight, but consider this—every voice matters, and when many are joined together, they can make a difference.

When Abercrombie released its 2003 Christmas catalog, chock-full of nude images and the phrase "Group Sex" included on the outer sleeve of the front cover, they apparently went too far even in our anything-goes culture. They ultimately pulled the catalog after a few weeks, saying they needed to make room on store counters for a new fragrance. My hunch tells me it had more to do with the more than three hundred phone calls an hour they received for days, the declining sales they reported in November and December, and the fact that several analysts downgraded their stock when they didn't meet their sales projections. They gambled on the marketing strategy that "sex sells" but learned the hard way that it ceases to sell when you cross that fine line and *offend* the buyers. I certainly respect that Christians have a right to shop at such stores, but for heaven's sakes, don't complain about our sex-crazed culture if you are helping keep some of the biggest abusers in business!

With the Internet it has never been easier to take a stand for virtue and let our voices be heard. Within five minutes of witnessing the controversial Super Bowl half-time show of 2004, I had e-mailed CBS off their Web site and their local affiliate station in my city. Minutes later when I saw an offensive ad that blasphemed the name of God, I e-mailed the company responsible. Several days later I received an e-mail apologizing for the ad, and it stated that they had decided to pull the ad after receiving numerous complaints. I also receive e-mail notices from several groups who are committed to tracking down the worst offenders of morality and virtue. These groups do all the grunt work and even prewrite the e-mail objecting to the offense in question. With a few clicks of my mouse, my objection is sent automatically to the powers-that-be. Some of my favorite sites are American Family Association's "Action Alerts" (www.afa.net) and www.onemillionmoms.com. You've heard it said, "Stand for something or you'll fall for anything." It's never been so easy to take a stand for virtue. Christians have no excuse to remain silent any longer.

I realize that many women may be somewhat hesitant to embrace the concept that a virtuous woman could have a feisty side to her when it comes to fighting for noble causes. In fact, I was amazed to discover that the actual Hebrew word used for "virtuous" in Proverbs 31:10—"Who can find a virtuous woman?" (KJV)—is *chayil*. It is used a total of 243 times in the Old Testament. Only three times, of the 243 times the word appears, is the English word *virtuous* used in its place. Most often when *chayil* is used, it is translated "army" (56 times) and "valour" or "valiant" (50 times). Other English words substituted for the word *chayil* are "host," "forces," "power," "might," "strength," and "strong." One verse where *chayil* is used is in 1 Samuel 16:18. It speaks of David before he became king and says:

> *One of the servants answered, "I have seen a son of Jesse of Bethlehem who knows how to play the harp. He is a brave man and a warrior [chayil]." (1 Sam. 16:18a)*

Don't you just love it? A virtuous woman is a strong, mighty, and valiant force. She is a warrior for righteousness. She would never settle for the world's counterfeit brand of strength called "empowerment." Her strength comes from God and not herself. Mighty women of God, let's unite for the cause of virtue and enter the battle. It's time to take back this virtueless culture for Christ. *Chayil!*

Thinking in Third Person

Chapter 5	I wonder if the Proverbs 31 woman would feel the same

twinge of guilt that most of us do when we meet the gaze of the beggar at the intersection holding a cardboard "will work for food" sign. Would she dig deep in her purse or avert her eyes and wait expectantly for the light to turn green? Would she answer the pleas of every charity that called during the dinner hour or offer a polite "We gave at the office"? Would she cheerfully write a check to the multitude of teenagers requesting assistance for their summer mission trips? What about the needy juveniles peddling gift wrap, Girl Scout cookies, and booster club discount cards? Did she extend her hands to every needy person and every needy cause that crossed her path?

I was surprised to discover that the meaning of the original Hebrew word used for "poor" is *'aniy* (aw-nee'), and it means "depressed in mind or circumstances." The

Hebrew word for "needy" is *'ebyown* (eb-yone'), which means "a sense of want; destitute." A modern-day definition would be "beggar" or "poor man." When you include "depressed in mind or circumstances" and "destitute" to the "poor and needy" category, the task becomes overwhelming. We have no lack of people who are physically, emotionally, and spiritually poor. What then is the balance in extending our hands to the needy around us? Needs will vary from person to person, and it's best to break down the needy into three categories.

Reaching Out to the Emotionally Needy

Years ago, when the Internet was a fast and growing phenomenon, the ministry I had started the year prior went online. We developed an online advice column as an anonymous forum for young women who were in need of answers. Before "spam" was a word in my vocabulary and, for that matter, an everyday annoyance, we took advantage of a marketing tool that would enable us to launch the site to the masses and drive those in need to our site. The text was very simple and said, "Facing a crossroads in life? We can help." We listed the link to our site and gave our friend with the mass mailing software the green light. The next morning I poised myself at my home computer in the kitchen, curious to see if any "crossroads" had been submitted to the advice column. I was shocked beyond belief to find hundreds upon hundreds of questions waiting in my inbox.

For days I weeded through the questions, looking first for the ones that were critical in nature. I immediately enlisted help from some God-fearing and wise Christian women who were willing to help answer the questions.

Even so, it hardly seemed to make a dent in the never-ending pile of needs that had landed in my inbox. I functioned off of little sleep as I replied to e-mails addressing thoughts of suicide, unwanted pregnancies, eating disorders, addictions, depression, sexual abuse, and other weighty issues. Many were way over my head, so I provided links to help lines, support groups, and reputable Christian counselors. I even arranged a suicide intervention at a teen girl's school in another state. I prayed and I wept over their situations. Never in my life had I been exposed to such a degree of desperate neediness. I was overwhelmed with the burden of responsibility I felt over the sheer fact that the crossroads of strangers had settled in my inbox, awaiting a sort of verdict. Who was I to be trusted with such an awesome responsibility? It awakened me to a world of hurt that I had not known existed. I had unknowingly wandered outside my safe cocoon and ventured into the world of neediness, albeit with a few strokes of my keyboard and an invitation to park your problems in my inbox.

As painful as the experience was, it would become a motivator for years to come as I served in ministry. God had offered me a glimpse of reality. In his wisdom, he also taught me several very important lessons about "extending my hands" to those with emotional needs. The first lesson that I learned was that I alone cannot save the world. I was grossly unqualified for the task—try as I may, in most situations I was unequipped to offer counsel. Second, I learned how my time spent addressing the needs of others quickly left me with little or no time to address the needs of my family. I accepted the sobering truth that God would not appoint me to a task if in the end it would leave my family with the short end of the stick. The final and most important lesson was that my ultimate goal in reaching out to the needy is to point them to God as the ultimate Healer and Comforter. Much is said in God's Word about our responsibility to "comfort" others, but nowhere does it footnote the command with an exhortation to fix their problems. Sometimes we have an obligation to reach out with more than just words of comfort, but other times our task is to "mourn with those who mourn" (Rom. 12:15).

When someone is emotionally needy, many have a tendency to attempt to fix the problem. A simple "I am so sorry you are experiencing that—can I pray for you?" is often more healing than a list of quick-fix solutions to the problem. This thought is especially convicting to me as a professional "know it all." I cringe at the thought of how many times I have offered advice and, heaven forbid, failed to even point them in God's direction. This is especially dangerous if our need to play the role of caretaker backfires and the one in need begins to depend on us and, as a result, is hindered from seeing God at work through the situation. God does not want us to place on our shoulders the burdens of the needy—that is his job. Often our job is to help them take the next step—by providing an empathetic and listening ear or by encouraging them to meet with their pastor or a professional counselor, depending on the situation. Do you sometimes become overly involved in meeting others' needs? Have you considered some specific ways to find balance in this area?

Just as many "overgive" to the needy, some give with impure motives. If the motive in giving is to produce an end result that would leave us glowing in the aftermath of "atta girls," we need to do a heart check. We need to remember 1 Corinthians 13:3 that says, "If I give all I possess to the poor and surrender my body to the flames, but have not love, I gain nothing." I wonder if perhaps Job's well-meaning friends had the wrong motive in mind when they set out to comfort him in his time of need. "Well-meaning" quickly transitioned into, well, just *mean!*

> When Job's three friends, Eliphaz the Temanite, Bildad the Shuhite and Zophar the Naamathite, heard about all the troubles that had come upon him, they set out from their homes and met together by agreement to go and sympathize with him and comfort him. (Job 2:11)

We are then told that upon seeing him, his friends wept aloud, tore their robes, sprinkled dust on their heads, and then sat down on the ground with him for seven days and seven nights in total silence "because they saw how great his suffering was" (v. 13). What a beautiful picture of what it is to mourn with those who mourn. Unfortunately, they failed to stop while they were ahead and finally opened their big mouths with all sorts of advice as to the "whys" behind his problems. Surely we can all think of times when we have shared a painful situation with someone only to be met with a speculative conclusion as to why we might be suffering. The last thing most of us want to hear in a time of hurt and loss is "God has a reason for everything," or "God works all things together for good." Sometimes all we can do is literally weep with someone and tell them in all honesty, "I don't know what to say." Job's friends were the model of comfort for seven days, but in the end they have been remembered for their untimely and unwelcome advice. With friends like that, who needs enemies!

Our primary responsibility in extending our hands to the emotionally needy is beautifully worded in 2 Corinthians 1:3–4:

> *Praise be to the God and Father of our Lord*
> *Jesus Christ, the Father of compassion and the*
> *God of all comfort, who comforts us in all our*
> *troubles, so that we can comfort those in any trou-*
> *ble with the comfort we ourselves have received*
> *from God.*

Even if others are comforted by our words or actions, we must never forget to give credit where credit is due. God alone is the Father of compassion and God of all comfort. What a relief to this former queen of fix-it-all. One verse that offers me comfort, and one that I have passed along to others in need of comfort, is Psalm 56:8: "You keep track of all my sorrows. You have collected all my tears in your bottle. You have recorded each one in your book" (NLT). I don't know of anything that offers more peace than to picture a God so attentive to our suffering that he collects each and every tear we shed in a bottle and logs the reason behind each tear in a book. No one can match that.

Reaching Out to the Physically Needy

> *Suppose a brother or sister is without clothes*
> *and daily food. If one of you says to him, "Go,*
> *I wish you well; keep warm and well fed," but does*
> *nothing about his physical needs, what good is it?*
> *(James 2:15–16)*

One need not look far to find the poor and destitute. We can all reflect on times when God has placed a need in our path, and it has been clear that we are to be part of his plan in meeting the need. That is not to assume that we are called to respond to *every* need we encounter. If we are honest, many of us would have to admit we are nothing more than seasonal givers when it comes to extending our hands to the physically needy. Christmas is our wake-up call to the fact that there are many who are much less fortunate than we are. When the physical needs of the poor are made public, we generally respond by rushing to fill the food pantries, sponsor needy families, and provide winter coats and blankets. Come December 26, we breathe a sigh of relief along with the rest of the general public, convinced that we have done our yearly good deed.

A virtuous woman is not a seasonal giver but a sees-all-year-round giver. She is aware that the poor and the destitute are unable to consign their neediness to the month of December. Consistent year-round giving is the end result of an attitude of the heart that acknowledges that our resources don't belong to us in the first place. God has allowed us the resources, and with that blessing comes a responsibility to be good stewards with what he has entrusted to us. Yet many of us, if we are honest, have felt that selfish tendency to keep our blessings to ourselves. A true test to determine our attitude in regard to the stewardship of the blessings God has bestowed upon us is in tithing. I read a disturbing statistic that only 6 percent of all Protestants tithe to their local churches.[1] If we are unable to part with the biblically mandated 10 percent of our income as required in Scripture, it is an indication that our hearts are not right when it comes to an attitude of year-round giving.

Our tithes enable our churches to operate and meet the needs of the congregation and others. Our offerings help directly meet the physical needs of others and should come over and above our tithe. I believe many Christians are unable to tithe and extend their hands to the needy because they have overextended their finances to meet their own perceived needs. Many sincerely want to give to others, but they find themselves entrapped in a vicious cycle of bills and expenses that barely meets or exceeds their income. Because they are not walking in obedience to God's plan, they are plagued by frustration and guilt.

If this is your situation, let me encourage you not to be overwhelmed with giving an entire 10 percent of your income if it seems impossible. Review your budget and look for things you can cut out. Start by giving an amount on a monthly basis, even if it is not 10 percent. Have the goal of working up to the 10 percent, and develop the willpower to say no to things that are not necessary. Even when you are regularly giving a percentage less than the required 10 percent, you are developing the consistent habit of giving year-round. Those who consistently tithe are perhaps the most giving people in the world because they have learned the discipline that their wealth was earned by God's hand and was meant to be dispensed accordingly, by his will. In Malachi 3:10 God tells the people, "'Bring the whole tithe into the storehouse, that there may be food in my house. Test me in this,' says the LORD Almighty, 'and see if I will not throw open the floodgates of heaven and pour out so much blessing that you will not have room enough for it.'"

This is the only verse in the Bible where God invites us to test him, yet many fail to take him up on the offer and miss the blessings he intended for them. In Malachi 3:8, God states that we rob him when we fail to bring our tithes and offerings. God knew that we would have a tendency to hang on to the blessings he bestows upon us. He also knew that in setting up the system of tithing and the giving of offerings, we would be reminded that he is the ultimate Provider of all things. It's a win/win for all involved—our giving meets the needs of the local church and the physical needs of others, and we feel the rest in our souls that comes with obedience. Truly, "it is more blessed to give than to receive" (Acts 20:35).

Even though I am faithful and consistent in giving a tithe to my local church as well as offerings over and above my tithe to meet the needs of others, I often feel convicted that I could do more. God is ever so patient with me as I wrestle with conviction over my frivolous spending on new shoes (ouch), grande lattes (double ouch), and clothes that sometimes never get worn (I'm feeling sick now). While God is a God of grace, and he desires for us to partake in certain pleasures, he wants us to have a healthy balance when it comes to our wants. When we keep the needs of others in the forefront of our minds, we tend to be less frivolous and wasteful with his resources. Ultimately, our attitude in giving should be such that our left hand does not know what our right hand is doing (Matt. 6:3).

Reaching Out to the Spiritually Needy

I love the story in Luke 5:17–20 where Jesus was teaching in a room filled with Pharisees and teachers of the law, and a paralytic man in need of healing was lowered on a mat through the roof. The crippled man's friends had attempted to take him into the house to lay him before Jesus, but the crowd prohibited them from doing so. In desperation, they resorted to what we call "drastic measures." I like to imagine what the scene looked like—Jesus is perhaps interrupted midsentence as all eyes were diverted to the ceiling where the dust and clay falling from above most likely announced the paralytic's grand entrance. Once on the ground, I wonder who broke the silence first. We are only told of Jesus' response, but it is likely that the friends made some attempt to explain their unusual action. The poor crippled man didn't have time to prepare a speech before the hastily hatched plan, although "I thought I'd drop in for a quick healing" would have been timely and honest. We don't know for sure what, if anything, was said prior to Jesus' unpredictable line, "Friend, your sins are forgiven" (v. 20), but it does not matter. Jesus eventually healed the man physically, telling him, "I tell you, get up, take your mat and go home" (v. 24), but he left little doubt as to the man's greatest need: spiritual healing.

When I was newly married and still a fairly new believer, I was invited to join a Christian women's group. I had been nominated by several friends and was initially enamored at the thought that I had been chosen to be a part of the group. I joined and paid the obligatory fee, was assigned a secret sister, and signed up for required community service hours. I chalked up hours gathering clothes for the poor and participating in a canned food drive yet began to feel a restlessness in my spirit over the fact that there seemed to be no formal strategy in place to share the gospel with the needy. I finally picked up the phone and called the president of the club and shared my concern. I was shocked when she replied that sharing the gospel was prohibited, as the goal was not to make anyone feel uncomfortable. She added that the mission of the organization was simply to meet the physical needs of the needy. I knew at that moment that this was not the club for me. I politely told her that I did not wish to invest my time in an organization that fails to take advantage of the wonderful opportunity to share the good news with the needy and resigned my membership.

I am in no way saying that the group did not accomplish worthy deeds in reaching out to the needy, but I felt that they missed some God-given opportunities to meet the spiritual needs of others. I shudder to think of the poor who, in spite of being fed and clothed in the name of Christ by many people and organizations, may someday find themselves at the threshold of heaven and hell having never been introduced to the great Provider.

Jesus emphasized the importance of caring for the poor throughout Scripture, but his final instructions to his disciples were to "go into all the world and preach the good news to all creation" (Mark 16:15). Final words are of utmost importance and indicate the priority that should be placed on tending to the spiritual needs of others. Many times we leave the evangelizing to those who are specifically called to be evangelists. For most, it is far more comfortable to minister to the poor in spirit than the spiritually poor.

A Christian's job title and job description can be found in 2 Corinthians 5:17–20:

> *Therefore, if anyone is in Christ, he is a new creation; the old has gone, the new has come! All this is from God, who reconciled us to himself through Christ and gave us the ministry of reconciliation: that God was reconciling the world to himself in Christ, not counting men's sins against them. And he has committed to us the message of reconciliation. We are therefore Christ's ambassadors, as*

though God were making his appeal through us.
We implore you on Christ's behalf: Be reconciled
to God.

Imagine how that would look on a business card with your name and your designated job title: "Ambassador for Christ"! As ambassadors, our job is to take the message of reconciliation to the people. That message of reconciliation is the good news that Christ has paid the penalty for our sins through his death on the cross. Those who believe on his name can stand before God with the righteousness of Christ, thereby being reconciled to him.

Over the years the word *evangelist* has become associated with flamboyant televangelists or street-corner preachers screaming at passersby to "get saved." The truth is, we are all called to be evangelists. Some are blessed with a boldness to share the good news with words while others are blessed with the ability to share the good news through deeds. In 1 Corinthians 3:6 Paul says, "I planted the seed, Apollos watered it, but God made it grow." So often we associate the word *evangelist* with the actual telling of the gospel. Many people in my life were faithful to "plant" and "water" seeds of God's truth in the years that led up to my decision. While I am grateful to the ones who *told* me about Christ, I am just as grateful to the ones who *showed* me Christ. We cannot make anyone accept Christ, but we can point them in his direction through our words and deeds. We can practice evangelism through book clubs, bunko parties, scrapbooking, business trips, or simply reaching out to others in the name of Christ. God will then see our efforts through to salvation.

We need to be on the lookout for those who are spiritually needy in our neighborhood, workplace, kid's activities, and other spheres of influence. Many Christian women are resistant to venture outside of their comfort zone of Christian friends. I, too, tend to cling to that which is familiar, avoiding uncomfortable and unpredictable situations. Yet God is constantly at work setting up divine appointments and expecting us to share the good news of the kingdom. I am often convicted over the opportunities I have clearly missed in my call to share the good news. How grateful I am that those who presented the gospel to me, whether in words or deeds, didn't miss their opportunity!

When it comes to extending my hands to the spiritually needy, I am particularly touched and motivated by the story of John Harper. Harper was a thirty-nine-year-old evangelist from England aboard the *Titanic* on that fateful night of April 14, 1912. When the ship struck an iceberg, John Harper kissed his six-year-old daughter good-bye, handed her to his niece, and put them aboard a lifeboat. He then turned and headed back toward the throng of desperate passengers along the deck, yelling, "Women, children, and unsaved into the lifeboats!" When he was forced into the frigid, icy waters of the Atlantic, he was seen swimming frantically to people in the water and leading them to Christ before they were overtaken by hypothermia.[2]

Four years after the *Titanic* went down, a young Scotchman rose in a meeting in Hamilton, Canada, and said, "I am a survivor of the *Titanic*. When I was drifting alone on a spar that awful night, the tide brought Mr. John Harper of Glasgow, also on a piece of wreck, near me. 'Man,' he said, 'are you saved?' 'No,' I said. 'I am not.' He replied, 'Believe on the Lord Jesus Christ and thou shalt be saved.' The waves bore him away; but, strange to say, brought him back a little later, and he said, 'Are you saved now?' 'No,' I said, 'I cannot honestly say that I am.' He said again, 'Believe on the Lord Jesus Christ, and thou shalt be saved,' and shortly after, he went down; and there, alone in the night, and with two miles of water under me, I believed. I am John Harper's last convert."[3]

John Harper lived out 1 Corinthians 9:16, when Paul said, "Yet when I preach the gospel, I cannot boast, for I am compelled to preach. Woe to me if I do not preach the gospel!" As virtuous women we are called to extend our hands to the needy. While it is important that we attend to the emotional and physical needs of others, first and foremost we should be concerned with the spiritual needs of others. We have the good news—woe to us if we do not preach the gospel.

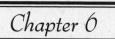

She can laugh at the days to come.

PROVERBS 31:25B

What Steals Your Joy?

Chapter 6

If it were possible to bottle up and sell the qualities that defined the Proverbs 31 woman, there is one in particular that could draw a line of women from all four corners of the globe. Her ability to "laugh at the days to come" would no doubt be at the top of every woman's list. The verse almost seems out of place in a passage otherwise shrouded by verses extolling the value of hard work. How refreshing to know that this woman actually took the time to *smile* in the midst of her busy day. It certainly hints at her emotional well-being to know that she could look to the future with confidence.

What enabled the virtuous woman of Proverbs 31 to trust in the days ahead without knowing what the days would hold? While we can't know for certain, she clearly had learned to avoid the "joy robbers" in life. John 10:10 reminds us that the thief comes to steal, kill, and destroy. Perhaps nothing gives Satan greater joy than to see God's children miss out on the abundant life during their earthly stay. If we are to possess the ability to laugh at the days to come, we must be sure to inoculate ourselves against joy robbers. Following are some common joy robbers that steal the laughter from many Christian women.

Joy Robber 1: When Life Doesn't Go According to Our Script

In his heart a man plans his course, but the LORD *determines his steps. (Prov. 16:9)*

When Keith and I were first married, he quickly established a five-year plan to organize our lives. The plan called for me to work full-time for several years before starting our family. This plan would enable us to save money for a house and get our feet on the ground financially.

The plan worked great for four months—until I discovered I was expecting a child. I'll never forget the morning I took the pregnancy test. Keith was out on the porch having his quiet time, no doubt pleading with God for the results to be negative. When I read the positive result on the test, I couldn't mask my elation and set out to share the good news. Even though I knew a baby wasn't part of the "plan," I somehow imagined that Keith, too, would be overjoyed with the news.

When I stepped out on the porch and shared that I was in fact pregnant, his first words were, "You can't be pregnant. We don't have a baby in the budget." A dozen roses later, all was forgiven, and we began to adjust to the new plan. In the budget or not, we had a baby on the way. We never expected to celebrate our first anniversary at a Lamaze class doing breathing exercises. Talk about romantic! Exactly thirteen months after we were married, our son, Ryan, was born. He may not have been part of our plan at that time in our lives, but I sure can't imagine life without him. How thankful I am that our perceived desires didn't get in the way of God's divine plan.

Can God interrupt our lives at any time and throw us off of our carefully plotted courses? You bet! We are so accustomed to plotting and planning our lives that we naturally assume God will follow closely behind, sprinkling magic fairy dust on our man-made plans. God certainly doesn't expect us to give up all planning for the future, but he wants us to find the balance of planning ahead while remaining flexible should he happen to steer our plans in a different direction. Too often we get consumed with our agenda and forget who is really in charge. Sometimes we fail even to run our desires past God to make sure they line up with his desires.

Many things that may seem or feel right to us, when lined up against the principles set forth in God's Word, are not right. If we "desire" a bigger home but the higher house payment would hinder us from tithing, don't even think about asking God to make it happen! If you are a single woman and in love with a man who is not a believer, don't ask God to bless the union! If your business dealings would compromise your integrity, don't ask God to help you close the deal! I am amazed at some of the stories women have shared with me over the years about how God supposedly gave them the "desires" of their hearts even though it would have clearly compromised his very principles set forth in Scripture. If we want to laugh at the days to come, we must give God his rightful place in the driver's seat of our lives. Women who fail to do so will experience restlessness in their souls over the conflict of interest between the will of the flesh and the will of the Spirit. When we fail to run our plans or desires past God or prioritize our desires above his will, we are basically saying, "God, I can't trust you with the reins of control in my life." Take it from someone who has learned the hard way—God is never content in the passenger's seat. When it comes to the perfect script, we trust him with the beginning and the end—why not the in-between?

Joy Robber 2: When We Base Contentment on Circumstances

Another joy robber that leaves women grumbling rather than laughing is the "if only" syndrome. Women suffering from this ailment have mistakenly allowed their circumstances to define their happiness or, in many cases, their misery. It is impossible to laugh at the days to come unless you are content with the day at hand.

Following are a list of common if-onlys I have heard from women through the years. If only . . .

- I was married.
- I wasn't married.
- my husband was a Christian.
- my husband was a spiritual leader.
- my children were obedient.
- my prodigal would return.
- I had a better job.
- I had a job.
- I made more money.
- I could get out of debt.
- I had a bigger house.
- I had a house.
- I was in good health.
- I could lose weight.
- I could meet the perfect guy.

- I could quit my job and stay home.
- I could go back to work.

Paul was no stranger to overcoming the if-only syndrome. He spoke with honesty and vulnerability when he said, "I am not saying this because I am in need, for I have learned to be content whatever the circumstances. I know what it is to be in need, and I know what it is to have plenty. I have learned the secret of being content in any and every situation, whether well fed or hungry, whether living in plenty or in want" (Phil. 4:11–12).

I am thankful for people like Paul in Scripture who give us the hope that we too can learn "the secret of being content in any and every situation." I speak firsthand as one whose laughter at the days to come hinged on a long list of if-onlys. The problem with attaching contentment to an if-only is that it is never-ending. No sooner do you conquer one if-only than there are a string of others following close behind. If-onlys never travel alone.

In fact, let me give you one of my opinions. I really suspect we will never be completely free of an occasional bout of the if-only syndrome. So what do you do with an attack of the if-onlys? I think the ultimate solution is to lift each one up to God and pour our hearts out to him. Philippians 4:6–8 provides God's remedy for trading our if-onlys for a calm and settled peace.

Do not be anxious about anything, but in everything, by prayer and petition, with thanksgiving, present your requests to God. And the peace of God, which transcends all understanding, will guard your hearts and your minds in Christ Jesus. Finally, brothers, whatever is true, whatever is noble, whatever is right, whatever is pure,

whatever is lovely, whatever is admirable—if any-
thing is excellent or praiseworthy—think about
such things. (Phil. 4:6–8)

Most people who suffer from the if-only syndrome also experience a chronic spirit of discontentment. The two ailments go hand in hand. Some people will find ways to cope with the frustration of chasing down one if-only after another, which complicates the matter even more. If you are discontent in your marriage and placating the pain by eating everything in sight, you have just created another if-only. If charging up your credit card helps you to solve one if-only but leaves you in debt, you have simply traded one if-only for another. Nothing will cure the if-only syndrome until you decide to be content in any and all situations. There is no sense in postponing your laughter when you can laugh today.

Joy Robber 3: Unrealistic Expectations

We've all experienced it. You invest untold hours into planning for the perfect family vacation only to discover that there is no such thing as a "perfect family vacation." My husband and I learned this truth the first time we took our kids snow skiing. All three were under the age of ten, and in hindsight, that should have been our clue that our expectations would not match up with reality. We had planned the trip with visions of happy children learning to ski for the first time, racing all the way down the mountain to ride the lift again and again. The vision continued with the family gathered around the fireplace at the end of the day, sipping hot cocoa in our cabin surrounded by picturesque snowcapped mountains. Yeah, right.

When we dreamed up the perfect family vacation, we failed to factor into our equation that it took half a day just to get the little tykes ready for the slopes. Once dressed, the fun continued with lost gloves, constant adjustments of boots that were too tight, and frequent trips to the bathroom, thus requiring us to undress and dress them again. An all-time favorite family memory caught on videotape was when our then seven-year-old daughter threw her body into the snow in front of the ski school and screamed at the top of her lungs for all on the mountain to hear, "You are the meanest parents in the world if you make me stay at this stupid ski school!" And all this occurred in the first hour on the slopes. My husband and I then spent the next several days on a bunny slope as flat as our driveway looking longingly up at the blue runs on the mountain that we were accustomed to skiing on past trips, sans the children. Keith's eyes glazed over every time he mentally calculated the cost per person per day to make memories on the bunny slope. By the time the trip was over, Keith and I both needed a vacation to recover from the vacation.

We're slow learners, and much like childbirth, the negative aspects of that trip had faded when years later we were off to the slopes again for yet another perfect family vacation. This trip yielded a pair of lost goggles somewhere between the parking lot and the ski lodge on day one, an injury on day two, a lost teenager on the slopes on day three, and our son announcing ten miles out of town as we were leaving on day four that he had left his retainer back in the cabin. Every vein was standing out on my husband's neck as he turned the car around to return to the cabin. You've heard the saying, "The family that prays together stays together." I recently heard a variation of the saying that says, "The family that skis together hates each other." Of course, it was meant to be tongue-in-cheek, and as a family that skis together, I could relate to the intended humor.

Overall we have wonderful memories of all of our family vacations, in spite of the fact that not one has yet to measure up to our preconceived expectations. Over the years we have learned to lighten up and flex with the obvious kinks that will come with our man-made plans. Our new motto on family vacations is "Choose your attitude." Not exactly what my husband wanted to hear on his way back to fetch the retainer, but good advice all the same. Our joy doesn't have to fade when our expectations fail to match up with reality or, for that matter, when the pictures in our photo albums fail to look like the pictures in the vacation brochures.

Joy Robber 4: When Our "Worst-Case Scenario" Becomes a Reality

Therefore do not worry about tomorrow, for tomorrow will worry about itself. Each day has enough trouble of its own. (Matt. 6:34)

I am a "recovering worrier," which translates into "I still worry but not as much as I used to." One thing I have learned to do whenever I find myself worrying over an event that might occur in the future is to attack it head-on by imagining the "worst-case scenario" as the outcome. While this may seem depressing to some, I actually find it very helpful. Rather than torture myself wondering if what "might be" will actually come to be, I walk through the worst-case scenario in my mind. This may seem like a simple anecdote for worry, but it works for me. Case in point: my current "worry du jour" is about my daughter starting public high school after having been at the same private Christian school since kindergarten. It was a mutual parent-child decision, but it did not come easily. She is leaving behind a solid peer group of girls, many of whom she has known since kindergarten. She will go from a class of fifty students to a class of six hundred students, and the worst part is that she knows no one in her grade. Even though the first day of school is six months away, I have thoroughly tortured myself with visions of her sitting at the lunch table by herself day after day, week after week, month after month. Finally, I decided to apply my "worst-case scenario" methodology to the situation. I imagined the very worst situation—she goes to school and, sure enough, sits alone at the lunch table. Yet as I walked myself through the possibilities, I concluded that should she struggle to make new friends, it would provide her with an opportunity to trust Jesus and lean on him. Once I had come to terms with what "might be" and pictured myself and my daughter in that situation, the problem didn't seem nearly as insurmountable as I had imagined.

Now I realize that my worry over what "might be" when my daughter attends a new school is trivial compared to some situations that leave others wondering what might be. I do not intend in any way to minimize some very real and painful situations that could bear out tragic results by offering a simple-sounding solution. I think of a friend who was just diagnosed with cancer and is now left wondering what might be should the treatments not work. I think of a friend whose husband is out of work and who wonders what might be should he not find work soon. I think of a friend who is struggling with infertility and the realization of what might be. I think of a friend who just discovered her husband has an addiction to porn. He has left her with their two children, and she is struggling with what might be.

Perhaps you are experiencing a very painful situation and are consumed with worry over what might be. Maybe you cannot imagine laughing at the days to come because you can't gather the strength to laugh—period. In a very short, unfamiliar book of the Bible, a prophet named Habakkuk experienced worry over sin, lawlessness, and injustice in Judah. He lodged a complaint to God, asking, "How long, O LORD, must I call for help?" and "Why do you make me look at injustice? Why do you tolerate wrong?" (Hab. 1:2a, 3a). God hears his complaint and gives Habakkuk an answer, but it is not the answer Habakkuk wants to hear. In fact, this is a worst-case scenario sort of answer. Habakkuk then goes before God again and lodges another complaint. God does not budge and restates his original sentence on the people of Judah. Habakkuk, the prophet, is given the devastating news that Judah will be destroyed at the hands of the Babylonians, a ruthless people "whose . . . strength is their god" (v. 11).

Like Habakkuk, we too are welcome to bring our complaints before God. He may or may not answer them in the way we would like, but he will not cast us out for asking, How do you respond when you don't get the answer you want? I'm sure Habakkuk wanted to scream from the top of his lungs, "It's not fair, Lord!" Have you ever said, "It's not fair, Lord!"? I know I have. How I wish I had learned earlier in my Christian walk to respond like Habakkuk to situations that bore unjust results. If you've never read his response before, sit down, because it will knock your socks off. Habakkuk's response to God after hearing the devastating news that what he worried "might be" would in fact become a reality was this:

> Even though the fig trees have no blossoms,
> and there are no grapes on the vine; even though
> the olive crop fails, and the fields lie empty and
> barren; even though the flocks die in the fields,
> and the cattle barns are empty, yet I will rejoice in
> the LORD! I will be joyful in the God of my salva-
> tion. The Sovereign LORD is my strength! He will
> make me as surefooted as a deer and bring me
> safely over the mountains. (Hab. 3:17–19 NLT)

Did you catch that?! "Even though . . . yet I will rejoice in the LORD!" What is your complaint today? Can you fill in the blank below and respond like Habakkuk?

"Even though _____

_____, yet I will rejoice in the Lord!"

Did your husband leave you for another woman? Are you out of work? Has one of your children broken your heart? Are you struggling with infertility? Have you been falsely accused of something? Has someone dear to you been diagnosed with a terminal illness? It is not my intent to minimize situations that are extremely hurtful. I am in no way implying that interjecting your complaint in the blank above will leave you with a sudden and miraculous dose of peace that surpasses all understanding. For some it might, but for most it will be an exercise of faith to say it aloud. Even if you cannot sincerely respond as Habakkuk did, I encourage you to claim it and ask God to help you believe it. Responding as Habakkuk did in the face of a worst-case scenario will be a process that if faithfully practiced will, over time, become a habit.

One Bible commentary had this to say about Habakkuk:

> He realized that inner peace did not depend on outward prosperity. Habakkuk did not state that he would merely endure in the hour of distress. He said he would **rejoice in the LORD** and **be joyful**. God is the inexhaustible source and infinite supply of joy. Far too many people keep trying to buy joy, but happiness is not found in circumstances. Joy is available to everyone, even to those stripped of every material possession, for joy is to be found in a Person. It comes through an intimate and personal relationship with the Lord, so that even those in the worst circumstances can smile.[1]

I'm sure we can all think of some modern-day Habakkuks who, even in the worst circumstances, could still manage a smile. I have a feeling the virtuous woman of Proverbs 31 was one of these rare people. She must have settled the matter up front with God that no matter what the future would hold, she would never lose the ability to smile.

Joy Robber 5: When We Get Stuck on the "Whys" of Life

Horatio Spafford had every reason to get caught up in the "whys" of life. A friend of the famous evangelist D. L. Moody, Horatio Spafford planned a family vacation to England that was to include joining up with Moody to help him with one of his great evangelistic campaigns. Just before the family was to set sail, Spafford was detained on a business matter. Not wanting to delay the vacation, he sent his wife and four daughters ahead on the *Ville Du Havre* and agreed to follow days later when the business matter was settled. Sadly, on November 22, 1873, the ship was struck, and it sank in twelve minutes. Nine days later Spafford received a telegram from his wife that simply said, "Saved alone." He immediately set sail to join his grief-stricken wife. The captain of his vessel called him up to the bridge as they passed over the area where his four daughters had drowned.[2] Rather than lobby God with a series of whys, Spafford instead returned to his cabin and penned the words to the great hymn "It Is Well with My Soul."

> *When peace, like a river, attendeth my way,*
> *When sorrows like sea billows roll;*
> *Whatever my lot, Thou has taught me to say,*
> *It is well, it is well, with my soul.*

Are you able to say, "It is well with my soul," in the face of adversity, or instead, do you get caught up in the whys of life? Perhaps one of the greatest signs of maturity in the Christian is the ability to respond to adversity with "It is well with my soul." While it is impressive enough that Horatio Spafford had the maturity to write the words to this beloved and classic hymn in the midst of great tragedy, it is all the more impressive considering the tragedies he had endured prior to losing his four daughters. Just two years before he had lost much of his fortune in the Great Chicago Fire of 1871. One year before that he had lost his only son to scarlet fever. Knowing these facts sheds greater understanding on his ability to write the words, "Whatever my lot, Thou has taught me to say." No doubt, he could have lobbied God endlessly with a series of angry whys. Instead, he clung to God and learned to trust him, even when life didn't make sense.

Little is said of Horatio Spafford's wife, Anna, but her faith in God was equally as notable as her husband's. Anna Spafford had stood bravely on the deck with her daughters—Annie, Maggie, Bessie, and Tanetta—clinging desperately to her. Her last memory was that of her baby being torn violently from her arms by the force of the waters. Anna was saved from the fate of her daughters by a plank that floated beneath her unconscious body, propping her up. When the survivors of the wreck had been rescued, Mrs. Spafford's first reaction was one of complete despair. Then she heard a voice speak to her: "You were spared for a purpose." She immediately recalled the words of a friend: "It's easy to be grateful and good when you have so much, but take care that you are not a fair-weather friend to God."[3]

What counsel that is for those of us who desire to be virtuous women! If we are to develop the habit of laughing at the days to come, we must take heed that we do not become fair-weather friends to God during times of adversity. If you are one who must know why, you will drive yourself mad waiting for an explanation from God. There are many things in this life that no matter how much energy we pour into understanding the why behind the matter, we will never find a valid explanation. Some things were never meant to be disclosed this side of heaven.

Isaiah 55:9 reminds us: "As the heavens are higher than the earth, so are my ways higher than your ways and my thoughts than your thoughts."

Have you come to terms with the truth that God's ways are higher than man's understanding? The story is told that when the Spaffords eventually met up with D. L. Moody, Horatio Spafford said to his friend, "It is well; the will of God be done." Have you accepted that

God is God and you are not? He does not owe us an explanation for anything. James 1:2–4 gives us the secret to true Christian maturity: "Consider it pure joy, my brothers, whenever you face trials of many kinds, because you know that the testing of your faith develops perseverance. Perseverance must finish its work so that you may be mature and complete, not lacking anything."

The Greek word for "joy" is *chara,* which means "cheerfulness" or "calm delight." Can you imagine having a faith so radical that you could almost respond to trials with "Yippee! It's training time again!" I certainly have a long way to go, but I desperately want to have a radical faith.

Praise God that Paul didn't get caught up in the whys of life over his thorn in the flesh (2 Cor. 12:7). Or what about Jesus? He could have easily asked God, "why?" on his way to suffer on the cross, but instead he said, "Father, if you are willing, take this cup from me; yet not my will, but yours be done" (Luke 22:42). Have you allowed the whys of life to stifle your ability to laugh at the days to come?

When my kids were young, they loved to play the trust/fall game—the one where I would stand behind them and they would fall backwards into my arms. I noticed that the older they got, the less they trusted that I would catch them. You would think that the older they got, the more they would rely on past experience and know that I would be there to catch them. When we struggle as Christians, we are, in a sense, playing the trust/fall game with God.

The Proverbs 31 woman knew God loved her and had her best interests in mind. She never doubted that he was in control of every detail of her life, *even* when life made little sense. When playing the trust/fall game with God, she didn't preoccupy herself with whether he would be there—she knew he would because he had always been there in times past. With confidence she never glanced back.

Laughing One Day at a Time

Have you allowed one or more of the "joy robbers" to steal your laughter? If so, it is never too late to make a change. Believe it or not, studies have actually proven that laughter can improve your health—physically, spiritually, and emotionally. Proverbs 17:22 confirms what many professionals are just now discovering: "A cheerful heart is good medicine." When was the last time you had a really good laugh? Didn't it feel good? The Bible advocates laughter as a part of our lives, yet we often allow the seriousness of life to quench our laughter. Each and every day will provide us with numerous opportunities to laugh. And while you're at it, learn to laugh at yourself. Lighten up when you fall short of perfection—everyone will make mistakes in life. While it is important to learn from our mistakes, it is equally important to laugh at our shortcomings along the way.

The virtuous woman of Proverbs 31 appears to have come to a place in her life where she trusted God with a calm, settled peace, and no matter what life brought her way, she determined never to stop laughing. If we are to laugh at the days to come, we must first learn to laugh at the day at hand.

For wisdom is more precious than rubies,
and nothing you desire can compare with her.

PROVERBS 8:11

Wisdom Is a Girl's Best Friend

Chapter 7

I'll never forget the first time I heard the name Ada Ferguson. My friend and pastor's wife, Carolyn, had been invited to be part of a small group meeting weekly in Ada's kitchen. For weeks Carolyn went on and on about Ada Ferguson and the godly wisdom she possessed. Finally I could stand it no longer. I asked to join the group. I mean, why not? I could certainly use a little wisdom in my life. Prior to the first meeting, I was a little apprehensive and not sure what to expect. I pictured an elderly woman with gray hair swept up in a bun, reading Scripture aloud from a big King James Bible, emphasizing the thees and thous.

Nothing could prepare me for the first meeting. When Ada answered the door, she was nothing like my image of a woman of wisdom. She was beautiful, stylish, and had a haircut to die for. She didn't seem old enough to possess wisdom. She immediately put me at ease, and we all gathered around her kitchen table with coffee in hand. She prayed with ease and comfort, as if she was accustomed to spending many hours at the throne of God. She spoke to the Father with reverence, praising him for our husbands and our responsibility as mothers to raise our children as godly seed for the next generation.

It quickly became clear that Ada Ferguson knew God's Word backward, forward, sideways, and upside down. Whether we were talking about husbands, kids, politics, decorating, or mothers-in-law, Ada always seemed to have morsels of truth from God's Word. She could take the Scriptures and make them come alive. Her comments were always spoken with confident authority, laced with wisdom, and shared in a spirit of humility. She was not puffed up with knowledge of Scripture but desperately dependent on walking with Christ on a daily basis. She was sensitive to sin in her life and would grieve over missed opportunities to share the love of Christ or over her children's friends who did not know the Lord. She spoke with compassion for everyone, never speaking in harsh judgment.

It was clear from the beginning that at the center of Ada's life was her relationship with Christ. The depth of her relationship with the Savior defined her role as wife, mother, friend, and mentor. Ada looked forward to time alone with God, and she got up early in the morning to meet with him. She also looked for ways to please and support her husband and children. Her countenance reflected that she lived a fulfilling and abundant life.

Ada shared that though she had been a Christian for many years, she did not really understand what it meant to make Christ the Lord of her life until her oldest child was two years old. At the time Ada's husband was not a

Christian, and she adopted 1 Peter 3:1–6 as her life verses. She was committed to winning her husband to faith in Jesus Christ without preaching or nagging. Nearly three decades later Ada's faithfulness was rewarded, and her husband walked forward in a worship service one Sunday morning and gave his life to Christ. God drew him that morning, but Ada's commitment years prior played a large part in his name being added to the Book of Life. God honored Ada's faithful obedience and her pursuit of godly wisdom. Today Ada and her husband minister together in their local church.

The more time I spent with Ada, the more it whet my appetite to pursue godly wisdom. Ada's wisdom did not come from a knowledge of the "wise" teachings of Socrates, Aristotle, or Plato. Her crown of wisdom came as a result of her priority of spending time alone with God.

> *Likewise, teach the older women to be reverent*
> *in the way they live, not to be slanderers or*
> *addicted to much wine, but to teach what is good.*
> *Then they can train the younger women to love*
> *their husbands and children, to be self-controlled*
> *and pure, to be busy at home, to be kind, and to*
> *be subject to their husbands, so that no one will*
> *malign the word of God.* (Titus 2:3–5)

I am thankful for the years I spent meeting across Ada's kitchen table. In Titus 2:3–5, older women in the faith are encouraged to train the younger women. If you have never had the privilege of meeting on a regular basis with an older godly woman, I encourage you to consider it. I'm not suggesting that you become dependent on a person, but I am suggesting that wisdom begins with a teachable spirit.

Depending on where you are today in your relationship with God, be sensitive to the fact that he may be leading you to be the "older woman" in someone else's life. I have had the privilege of leading several groups of college women in years past, and I have always come away blessed by their teachable spirits. I know firsthand the benefits of being on the receiving end of a godly teacher and role model. I am so intensely grateful for Ada's godly influence in my life. Now, wherever I minister, a part of Ada ministers with me. I can only imagine the joy around the throne when Ada sees her reward.

Wisdom Is More Than Knowledge

Before we attempt to acquire the godly virtue of wisdom, we must first make a distinction between wisdom and knowledge. *Knowledge* is a body of information: facts and figures. *Wisdom,* on the other hand, is good judgment: knowing what to do with knowledge.

I told you about Ada. She doesn't just possess knowledge of the Bible; she has biblically guided judgment that comes from many hours logged sitting at the feet of the Lord.

From the moment we are born, we begin to store up knowledge. In school the goal is to obtain as much knowledge as possible. We are applauded for good report cards, honors classes, honor roll, and graduating at the top of our class. When we get to college, honor students are a dime a dozen, and those who have no desire for knowledge are quickly weeded out.

For the foolishness of God is wiser than man's wisdom, and the weakness of God is stronger than man's strength. (1 Cor. 1:25)

My husband, Keith, possesses great knowledge. He graduated first in his college class in chemical engineering and received many honors for academic achievements. During his entire four years of college, he only made one B. Last I checked, there was a word to describe someone that smart—*NERD!* OK, maybe I'm a bit jealous (as someone who was rather excited about my *one* B!). One of his greatest honors came when he was chosen as one of fifty students, out of approximately fifty thousand, to receive a Presidential Scholarship. As part of the selection process, Keith and the other candidates had to go before a panel consisting of the dean of each college at the University of Texas. Each of the deans asked a challenging question to gauge the knowledge of each student. The process was grueling and intimidating, with the deans seated in a semicircle facing each student.

One of the deans asked Keith, "To what do you attribute your knowledge?" Keith responded, "My knowledge is a gift from God, and without him it would be worthless." He went on to share his testimony and emphasized that his faith in Christ was far more important than knowledge. As the deans stared back with shock and disapproval, Keith thought, *I just blew a scholarship.* However, on the way back to his dorm, he felt a calm and settled peace after having testified to the truth. To this day Keith believes God gave him the scholarship because of his faithfulness in answering the question. My husband is gifted with knowledge, but more importantly he is gifted with wisdom.

As the Scriptures say, "I will destroy human wisdom and discard their most brilliant ideas."
(1 Cor. 1:19 NLT)

Is wisdom a spiritual gift that only a few Christians will possess? No! James 1:5 reminds us that "if any of you lacks wisdom, he should ask God, who gives generously to all without finding fault, and it will be given to him." When you pray, are you in the habit of asking God for his wisdom?

The apostle Paul wrote to the church at Colosse, "Since the day we heard about you, we have not stopped praying for you and asking God to fill you with the knowledge of his will through all spiritual wisdom and understanding" (Col. 1:9). Wisdom comes through prayer and a life spent in relationship with God. Ecclesiastes 2:26 says, "To the man who pleases him, God gives wisdom, knowledge and happiness, but to the sinner he gives the task of gathering and storing up wealth to hand it over to the one who pleases God."

The knowledge the world emphasizes is very different from the type of knowledge God's Word emphasizes. The world considers knowledge something attained for pride, success, and advancement. Scripture says the knowledge of the truth leads to godliness (Titus 1:1). The world thinks knowledge originates with our human efforts, but the Bible tells us that God "made his light shine in our hearts to give us the light of the knowledge of the glory of God in the face of Christ" (2 Cor. 4:6).

Actually, we do agree with the world in one respect. The world thinks knowledge will open doors to meet our needs. We know through Scripture that God "has given us everything we need for life and godliness through our knowledge of him who called us by his own glory and goodness" (2 Pet. 1:3). Obviously, knowledge is not a bad thing as long as it is partnered with wisdom and used responsibly. It is far easier to gain knowledge alone than to obtain both wisdom and knowledge.

In the pursuit to become a virtuous woman, we need to obtain both wisdom and knowledge from the Holy One. Wisdom is the quality that makes the virtuous woman a rare find, with worth far above rubies. Many women will possess knowledge, but only few will possess wisdom. The world may esteem the pursuit of knowledge, but God honors the pursuit of godly wisdom.

> *Listen, my son, to your father's instruction and*
> *do not forsake your mother's teaching. They will*
> *be a garland to grace your head and a chain to*
> *adorn your neck.* (Prov. 1:8–9)

Wisdom: A Precious Jewel

Throughout the Bible, wisdom is often compared to gold, silver, or precious stones. The Book of Proverbs says, "Wisdom is more precious than rubies, and nothing you desire can compare with her" (8:11). It says to get wisdom is much better than to get gold (16:16). Look at what Job says of wisdom:

> *It cannot be bought with the finest gold,*
> *nor can its price be weighed in silver.*
> *It cannot be bought with the gold of Ophir,*
> *with precious onyx or sapphires.*
> *Neither gold nor crystal can compare with it,*
> *nor can it be had for jewels of gold.*
> *Coral and jasper are not worthy of mention;*
> *the price of wisdom is beyond rubies.*
> *The topaz of Cush cannot compare with it;*
> *it cannot be bought with pure gold.*
> (Job 28:15–19)

I still remember my first jewelry box. It was white with pink flowers. When you opened the lid, it would play music and a ballerina would twirl around. My love of jewelry started when I was a little girl. I would feed quarters into the gumball machine at the grocery store until I was rewarded with a jewelry trinket. As I got older, it didn't take long for me to figure out the difference between a cubic zirconium and a real diamond.

Never did I imagine, however, that I would someday be up to my ears in diamonds. Now before you jump to any conclusions, let me explain. When I was a college student, I had a part-time data entry job for a diamond broker. As my friends began to get engaged, I offered to sell them the diamonds for their rings at a price well below retail.

What began as a part-time job and a favor to help out a few friends eventually grew into a thriving home-based business. I developed accounts with diamond brokers across the country to ensure that my customers got the best price. It was a sweet deal, for I never had to buy any inventory. Brokers would mail me diamonds when I needed them, and whatever didn't sell was simply mailed back. When it comes to diamonds, I have seen it all. I have sold diamonds of all shapes and sizes, some as large as three carats. My kids grew up watching mom sell diamonds across the kitchen table and thought nothing of it. In fact, when my youngest child, Hayden, was four years old, he had a friend over to play while I happened to be showing diamonds to a customer. When his friend asked him what I was doing, Hayden said, "Selling diamonds— doesn't your mom sell diamonds?"

What's amazing, however, is that the more diamonds I saw, the less I wanted them for myself. (My husband will tell you that having the business was worth that revelation alone.) As I looked at diamond after diamond, up close and personal at 10-power magnification to identify their inherent flaws, I became aware of how imperfect they are.

I have since retired from the business and concluded that wisdom is far more valuable than jewels.

The virtuous woman would be far wiser to befriend the flawless gift of godly wisdom. It is far more valuable than any jewelry trinket money can buy, yet few will acknowledge that wisdom is a girl's best friend. Most women expend more energy longing for the world's baubles than pursuing this priceless treasure offered by God.

Better yet, it won't cost you a dime! The virtuous woman has worth far above rubies because she has chosen to adorn herself with wisdom rather than rubies, or for that matter, diamonds.

Think about your most prized possession from your jewelry box. Is it some item of great monetary value, or is it more an emotional treasure because of some memory attached? You probably have considered to whom you will one day hand it down. Would that item be as valuable as a legacy of wisdom? What can you do to see that when others look back on your life, they will say you valued wisdom over the baubles contained in your jewelry box?

The Rewards of Wisdom

If you are wise, your wisdom will reward you;
if you are a mocker, you alone will suffer.
(Prov. 9:12)

Like my dear sister Eve learned in the garden, I too learned the hard way that there are no shortcuts to obtaining wisdom. Early in my marriage Keith and I were looking to purchase a house. We prayed and asked God to give us wisdom to make the right decision. Shortly thereafter we found a house we liked, but it had escalating mortgage payments. Keith saw red flags all over the deal, while I saw vaulted ceilings and a master bathtub big enough to swim laps in.

I allowed my feelings to take over and convinced my sweet husband that God had led us to the house. (Hmmm. Do I recall Eve pulling the persuasion stunt, as well?) The house became a painful lesson with a high price. Fortunately, we were able to sell the place two years later. Because of that experience, we exercised better judgment when buying our next house.

I made the mistake of treating wisdom like an item in a vending machine. Just put your quarter in and out it comes. James 1:5 says that if we lack wisdom, just ask and God will give it liberally, right? I made the mistake of assuming that God will answer according to my time constraints and my feelings. True wisdom develops over time and comes as a result of walking with God on a regular basis. In a nutshell, godly wisdom is "thinking like God." We cannot think like God unless we know him by walking with him regularly.

Like me, have you had an experience when you prayed for wisdom but instead made the decision based on your human emotions and feelings? We could all learn a real lesson from Proverbs 2:12. It says, "Wisdom will save you from the ways of wicked men, from men whose words are perverse." Wisdom can, and at times has, saved me from my greatest threat of all—me.

While we're on the subject, look at some of the benefits of wisdom:

Do not forsake wisdom, and she will protect you;
love her, and she will watch over you.
Wisdom is supreme; therefore get wisdom.
Though it cost all you have, get understanding.
Esteem her, and she will exalt you;
embrace her, and she will honor you.
She will set a garland of grace on your head
and present you with a crown of splendor.
(Prov. 4:6–9)

Solomon said that wisdom would result in reward, praise, and hope.

If you are wise, your wisdom will reward you.
(Prov. 9:12)

A man is praised according to his wisdom.
(Prov. 12:8)

Know also that wisdom is sweet to your soul;
if you find it, there is a future hope for you,
and your hope will not be cut off.
(Prov. 24:14)

Did you see that last verse? Wisdom is a dessert with *no* calories! If you think that one's good, try this one:

Wisdom brightens a man's face and changes its
hard appearance. (Eccl. 8:1)

While the celebrities shell out the big bucks for Botox treatments that yield them frozen smiles, I'm going for the age-defying treatment recommended by the Great Physician.

The Folly of Fools

Many Scriptures in Proverbs contrast wisdom and folly. Webster defines *folly* as "the state of being foolish;

want of good sense, or weakness." Here is what the book of Proverbs says:

> *Folly is loud . . . undisciplined and without*
> *knowledge.* (Prov. 9:13)
>> *Folly entices others to sin.* (Prov. 9:14–18)
>> *The mouth of a fool invites ruin.*
> (Prov. 10:14)
>> *The folly of fools is deception. (Prov. 14:8)*
>> *A fool's eyes wander to the ends of the earth.*
> (Prov. 17:24)
>> *He who trusts in himself is a fool.*
> (Prov. 28:26)

James points out one attribute that most indicates wisdom—"deeds done in . . . humility" (James 3:13). Now I know "deeds done in humility" don't come easy, but when I seriously look at the folly that is our human nature, and when I consider the consequences, I cry out, "Please, Lord, save me from myself. Teach me wisdom by walking with you."

> *Wisdom is found on the lips of the discerning,*
> *but a rod is for the back of him who lacks judg-*
> *ment.* (Prov. 10:13)

One of the best examples in Scripture of the contrast of wisdom and folly is the story of Abigail and her husband, Nabal. Ironically, Nabal's name means "fool" or "wicked." First Samuel 25 tells the story. Nabal was a very wealthy man. His wife, Abigail, was an intelligent and beautiful woman. Scripture says that Nabal, a Calebite, was "surly and mean in his dealings" (v. 3).

David was a fugitive from Saul. Word of David's strength had gotten out, and many, including Abigail, speculated that the Lord would someday appoint him leader over Israel. While in hiding from Saul, David settled in the Desert of Maon and eventually found himself and his followers in need of food and provisions. David sent ten of his men to Nabal, a wealthy man living nearby, to solicit provisions. David's men had provided protection to Nabal's shepherds. The customs of the day dictated that Nabal assist David.

David instructed his men to say:

*Now I hear that it is sheep-shearing time.
When your shepherds were with us, we did not
mistreat them, and the whole time they were at
Carmel nothing of theirs was missing. Ask your
own servants and they will tell you. Therefore be
favorable toward my young men, since we come at
a festive time. Please give your servants and your
son David whatever you can find for them.*
(vv. 7–8)

When David's men arrived and made the request for provisions, Nabal not only refused to send provisions, he also attacked David's character, implying that he was an escaped slave. So David's men returned empty-handed and with news of the character attack Nabal had launched on him.

Think about the situation for a moment. David was the strongest fighting man in Israel. He had won many battles against several foes by this time. David had also been putting up with the murderous treatment of the insanely jealous King Saul for years. Does this sound like someone you would want to insult?

David didn't take the news well. He told his men to buckle on their swords, and he put on his. I would have hated to be Nabal's life-insurance underwriter about this time. Abigail entered the picture when one of the servants told her the story of Nabal's refusal to help David and his men. The servant told Abigail of the protection David and his men had provided them in the past. The servant showed far more wisdom than his master, Nabal. He appealed to Abigail: "Now think it over and see what you can do, because disaster is hanging over our master and his whole household. He is such a wicked man that no one can talk to him" (1 Sam. 25:17). Clearly, Nabal's folly had not gone unnoticed by the people.

Abigail responded to the servant's report by loading a large stock of provisions on donkeys and sending her servants ahead with provisions. She quickly followed behind.

Just before Abigail got to David, he had just said, "It's been useless—all my watching over this fellow's property in the desert so that nothing of his was missing. He has paid me back evil for good. May God deal with David, be it ever so severely, if by morning I leave alive one male of all who belong to him!" (vv. 21–22).

Upon hearing this, Abigail bowed humbly before David and made an appeal to him. She complemented David and assured him of God's faithfulness to someday appoint him leader over Israel. What were her motives in doing this? Abigail was an intelligent, God-fearing woman, and she was hoping to protect her household from David's wrath.

David blessed Abigail for her good judgment and for keeping him from bloodshed. David granted Abigail's request and sent her home in peace. I'm sure Abigail was experiencing mixed emotions on her way home. She must have felt tremendous relief having spared her household from death yet great sadness in having to return to a man as wicked as Nabal. Moreover, she was likely feeling somewhat fearful at the thought of sharing her whereabouts with Nabal.

When Abigail got home, Nabal was having a drunken party, so she once again used good judgment and waited until morning when Nabal was sober to tell him of the harm that almost came to his household. We do not know exactly what she said, but Scripture indicates she told him "all these things" (v. 37). It was then that Nabal's heart failed and he became like a stone. Ten days later the Lord struck (smote) Nabal and he died.

When David heard the news of Nabal's death, he praised the Lord for upholding his cause against Nabal and for bringing Nabal's wrongdoing down on his own head. He then sent his servants to Abigail with the purpose of asking her to become his wife. Abigail, still true to her character, bowed down with her face to the ground and said, "Here is your maidservant, ready to serve you and wash the feet of my master's servants" (v. 41). Keep in mind that wealth was no stranger to Abigail, yet she humbly gave herself to David.

Abigail is a wonderful example of someone who possessed much more than knowledge. Her testimony offers women the hope that in spite of negative circumstances, they can still become women of wisdom. Abigail's wisdom enabled her to endure an unhappy marriage when many would have become bitter. Not many women today could match Abigail's integrity. Most women faced with her situation would have bailed out a long time ago at the bidding of family, friends, and most marriage counselors. What a testimony in a time when divorces are a dime a dozen over "incompatibility" issues. The irony is that many in the world would call Abigail the "fool" for remaining in a bad marriage. Some may even applaud Nabal's aggressive business tactics and ability to accumulate wealth. Fortunately, Abigail was not in the habit of looking to the world for guidance. She was utterly dependent on God for her future and happiness, and as always, God rewarded her commitment to him. Abigail chose wisdom, while Nabal chose folly. In the end, wisdom and folly proved incompatible.

As you come to the end of this chapter, pray and ask God in faith—according to James 1:5—to give you wisdom. Ask him to make it the desire of your heart in your pursuit to become a virtuous woman.

She openeth her mouth with wisdom;
and in her tongue is the law of kindness.

PROVERBS 31:26 (KJV)

If You Can't Say Something Nice . . .

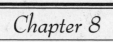

Chapter 8

It should come as no surprise that the Proverbs 31 woman had learned the art of "taming the tongue." In *The Message*, Eugene Peterson translates Proverbs 31:26: "When she speaks she has something worthwhile to say, and she always says it kindly." Ouch! Can we say that the majority of our conversations are "worthwhile" in nature and seasoned with godly wisdom? Just as important, are the majority of our words spoken in kindness? Double ouch. Verses like this one make me wonder why God appointed me to write this book. Remember that catchy slogan "Help! I've fallen and I can't get up"? I recently saw a T-shirt that read "Help! I'm talking and I can't shut up!" Some of us just have the gift of gab—or is it a gift? God keeps showing me that to speak with wisdom, I must first think before I speak. Proverbs 10:19 convicts me often: "When words are many, sin is not absent, but he who holds his tongue is wise."

I can't help wondering, did the Proverbs 31 woman ever have an off day? Did she ever get snippy with her husband when he refused to pull over and ask for directions? Was her voice still laced with kindness after holding on the phone for thirty minutes, waiting for tech support to straighten out her e-mail problems? Was it the classical music in the background that calmed her nerves?

Think of your most recent frustrating experience. How did you respond? Was the "law of kindness" on your tongue?

In Matthew Henry's Bible commentary, he says the following in regards to Proverbs 31:26: "Her wisdom and kindness together put a commanding power into all she says; they command respect, they command compliance. She is full of pious religious discourse, and manages it prudently, which shows how full her heart is of another world even when her hands are most busy about this world."[1]

The virtuous woman commands respect not as a result of an attitude but as a result of her speech, reflecting the true nature of her heart. Her very words "command compliance." I'll have to remember that one the next time I'm tempted to "command compliance" from my children using my standard method. Wisdom is rarely present in the midst of episodes where the veins on our necks are popping out while screaming at our kids to clean their rooms or get off the computer.

Here's a convicting thought. Can you think of three godly women who speak consistently with wisdom and kindness on their tongues? That was the easy part. Now, here's the punch line: Would your closest friends and family members think of your name when asked the same question? Certainly a convicting thought for many.

As I think of godly women who are in the habit of consistently speaking with wisdom and kindness, they all have one thing in common: each of these women exhibits a deep spirit of humility. Humility is an essential element in the pursuit to be a virtuous woman. The Hebrew word for "humility" is *'anavah,* which means "modesty, gentleness, and meekness." Displaying a spirit of humility comes naturally to someone who is in the habit of showing awe and reverence to God.

Someone who is humble understands that the only good in them comes as a result of the grace of God. They are grateful for each day that God grants them, and they view it as a privilege that he placed them in the world for such a time as this. They realize that as long as they live, they have more to learn. They extend grace and mercy to others because they realize the value of God's grace and mercy in their own lives. They are deeply dependent on God's Word, and prayer is a part of their everyday lives.

A Negative and Critical Spirit

Several godly women I know share testimonies to the fact that they used to be bitter in spirit until God's power and truth transformed their lives. Psychologists call it "behavior modification" while others refer to it as "the power of positive thinking." For the Christian it is called "living by the Spirit." This should offer hope to each of us that it's never too late to transform our speech. Luke 6:45 says, "For out of the overflow of his heart his mouth speaks." Are the majority of your words spoken from an overflow of a grateful heart? Are you in the habit of expressing an attitude of gratitude, or do you suffer from a negative and critical spirit?

As a past whine-aholic, I know firsthand the consequences of a negative and critical spirit. With the birth of my third child, I began to notice that more often than not, I viewed the glass as half empty rather than half full. This attitude was reflected in my speech, my countenance, and my actions. With three young children clamoring to have their needs met, at times I found myself short-tempered and resentful of my lot in life. God convicted my heart that should this habit continue, I was likely to grow into a bitter old woman. There was also the damaging effect too much whine would have on my own children. Whining, grumbling parents almost always raise whining, grumbling children who grow up to be whining, grumbling adults. It was time to break the cycle, and I pleaded for God's help.

My transformation did not happen overnight, but within months many around me noticed a change. I began to catch myself before responding, saying something positive instead. If my kids were driving me crazy, I stopped and thanked God for the blessing of being able to *have* children when so many cannot. If a tight budget prohibited me from affording the luxuries of life, I focused on what I did have rather than what I wanted. Eventually, dwelling on the positive became a habit. Today, I still must catch myself in certain situations that would normally elicit a string of bitter words. I still blow it from time to time, but I usually catch myself before I revert back to that negative and critical spirit that was demonstrated in my past days. Amazingly, when I revert back to my old ways, I can almost always link it to less time spent in prayer and reading God's Word.

If you struggle with being negative and critical, try the Whine-aholic's 5-Step Program:

1. Confess it to God and ask for his help.
2. Make prayer and reading God's Word a regular part of each day.
3. Make a concentrated effort to stop and think (or pray!) before you react or speak.
4. Try to rehearse at least one blessing for which to be grateful in circumstances where you find yourself feeling negative.
5. Ask someone to hold you accountable and ask you how you are doing in this area on a regular basis.

A virtuous woman thinks before she speaks, oftentimes determining that it is best not to speak at all. Sometimes the wisest thing to do is to remain silent. Most importantly, reflect on the greatest example of someone who consistently spoke with wisdom and kindness—Jesus. He could have easily spent his entire earthly ministry responding to what he witnessed among God's people with bitterness and harsh words yet instead he modeled grace and mercy.

Gossip and Hearsay

Though some tongues just love the taste of gossip, Christians have better uses for language than that. Don't talk dirty or silly. That kind of talk doesn't fit our style. Thanksgiving is our dialect.
(Eph. 5:4 *The Message*)

Most of us do not have to be convinced of the consequences of gossip. Scripture warns us over and over again to avoid gossip and to mind our own business. Why then do so many women, myself included, struggle to gain control of their tongues in this area? If you are female and breathing, you have likely been exposed (or at the helm!) of gossip within the past twenty-four hours. What is it that draws us like a magnet to the delicacies of forbidden gossip? Not God, that's for sure! Though we know it's wrong, it's as hard to resist as a hot Krispy Kreme doughnut on day three of our big diet. Rather than spend this part of the chapter in an attempt to convince you that gossip is wrong and, therefore, should be avoided, I am going to assume that most of us have drawn that conclusion.

First, let's clear the air by acknowledging that each of us has been guilty at one time or another of starting gossip, participating in gossip, or passing on hearsay. Whew, I know I feel better. Also, it would be unrealistic to assume that any one of us could successfully avoid being in the hearing of gossip in the future. Working along that premise, I am going to give some tangible ways to react to gossip and hearsay in the future.

Gossip is rarely preceded by a clear warning: "I am about to share gossip with you. Are you a willing party?" Most people are caught off guard and left with little time to react. The tasty forbidden morsels usually follow statements like:

"Did you hear . . ."

"I know I shouldn't say this, but . . ."

"Just between you and me . . ."

"If I tell you this, you have to swear . . ."

"I don't think she's shared it with many people . . ."

"I'm not sure she wants anyone to know, but . . ."

Ideally, it would be nice if we could head gossip off at the pass, but this is uncomfortable for many women, especially given the fact that most gossip is traded among friends. At a bare minimum, we should be able to respond with something to the effect of "I don't feel right about discussing this."

Listening to gossip is like eating cheap candy;
do you really want junk like that in your belly?
(Prov. 18:8 *The Message*)

As I have matured some in this area, I have at times caught myself saying some of the above phrases and stopping myself midsentence from continuing. Sometimes I blow it completely and end up feeling that familiar pang of conviction. I've heard it said that it constitutes gossip if you would not feel comfortable saying the statement in the presence of any of the subjects you discussed. If you are not part of the solution, then it serves no purpose to discuss the matter.

Hearsay differs from gossip in that it comes as third-hand (or more) information. Someone "hears" information and then "says" it to another without verifying the veracity of the statements. The old-fashioned game of gossip comes to mind, where a statement is whispered person to person until the last person receives the statement and then gives their version of the statement. Very rarely does the final statement match the original statement. Words are dropped along the way and other words are added until the statement is basically unrecognizable. A legal definition of hearsay is "evidence based on the reports of others rather than the personal knowledge of a witness and therefore generally not admissible as testimony."[2]

If hearsay is not allowed in a court of law, why would we even give it a second thought when it comes our way? Likewise, the information should not be admissible when it comes to making a judgment about the situation. As someone in ministry, I have had the unpleasant occasion of being a victim of hearsay on several occasions. By the time the absurd and sometimes devastating misinformation reached me, it had left a swath of damage in its wake. Many times the hearsay that was passed along was so ridiculous that were it not for the seriousness of it all, it would almost be laughable.

Had any one of the recipients of the hearsay taken the time to come to me directly for verification, it would have avoided much confusion and heartache. Each guilty party who failed to verify the statements and, instead, continued to pass along the morsels of mistruth took part in a plan orchestrated by an enemy bent on a mission to steal, kill, and destroy. Because of my experience as a victim of hearsay and the helpless feeling that comes with not being able to defend yourself against false information, I am now cautiously leery of hearsay that comes my way concerning others. I know firsthand the hurt that can result from being a victim and, as a result, would never want to be a player in a game that Satan plays all too well.

On the other hand, I have experienced situations where confirmed hearsay has provided me with useful information. The key, of course, is that it is *confirmed*. Sometimes information has been shared with me that, had I not known, could have led me to make an unwise decision. An example of this occurred early in my ministry when I was interested in booking a particular worship leader at a teen girl's event. I had listened to her music and felt that she would relate well with the teen girls. She was cute, hip, young, and newly married. However, when I mentioned to a youth minister friend that I was considering booking this young lady, he tipped me off that he had "heard" that she had become pregnant out of wedlock before she married and had the baby. His purpose was not to pass along juicy gossip but, rather, to inform me of a critical detail that, if true, could impact my decision. Rather than pass along the information to others as hearsay, I called her agent directly and asked if there were any grounds to the rumor. He confirmed it, and as a result, it led to my decision not to use her at the time. Even though this young lady was extremely repentant, I felt it was too early into her healing process to take a chance, especially at an event where young, impressionable teen girls might want to emulate her behavior upon seeing her apparent happy ending.

Let me also caution mothers that should we "hear" something pertaining to one of our children or their friends that could head off potentially damaging consequences, we have a responsibility to verify the information and take the proper course of action. The key factor in differentiating idle hearsay from useful information is whether it serves a purpose. If I spot a friend's child entering an R-rated movie at the theater, drinking alcohol, driving recklessly, or participating in any other activity that could bring themselves or others harm, I have a responsibility to inform the parents of what I have witnessed. If I "hear" the above information from someone else, I have a responsibility to encourage the one bringing the information to contact the parents rather than pass along gossip that serves little purpose. It is not necessary for multitudes of people to be involved. Too often we mothers have a tendency to participate in hearsay regarding other kids that serves no fruitful purpose. Again, should we be on the receiving end of such gossip, we should stop and ask ourselves and the parties involved if it serves a purpose to be discussing the matter.

There is a difference between useful information that serves a direct purpose and idle gossip and hearsay. A virtuous woman will be able to discern between the two. I have taught my daughter that if she often finds herself on the receiving end of gossip, she has likely been perceived by others as a willing participant. How about you? Do you steer clear of gossip and hearsay, or do you often find yourself initiating or participating in idle talk? If so, it's never too late to ask God to help you change your ways.

Let your conversation be always full of grace, seasoned with salt, so that you may know how to answer everyone. (Col. 4:6)

Words That Promote Healing

Perhaps one of the most irresponsible uses of our words is when we use them as weapons against others. It was unbecoming in junior high, and it is even more so in adulthood. The motive is almost always linked to that cathartic, yet fleeting, feeling that comes with trashing someone else so we can feel better about ourselves. This habit is especially unbecoming when mothers trash other kids to feel better about their own kids—some even in the hearing of their children! What is it about women that leaves us feeling threatened if someone else or someone else's children prosper? One of the most difficult, yet rewarding, things we can learn is the art of rejoicing with those who rejoice (Rom. 12:15). An inability to rejoice with those who rejoice exposes an insecurity within us that implies we are unable to fully accept that our worth (or our children's worth) is defined in Christ rather than by the shallow standards set forth by the world.

Some people make cutting remarks, but the words of the wise bring healing. (Prov. 12:18 NLT)

Ashamedly, I must admit to a time in my life when, due to my own insecurities, I was in the habit of making harsh, cutting remarks about others. As I began to accept that my worth was in Christ, the negativism began to subside. I still am tempted from time to time, but I now recognize that the problem lies with me and not with the victim of my careless words. When I am tempted to speak harshly against another, a good exercise for me has been to say something positive about the person instead.

A virtuous woman does not waste her time on the telephone hashing out whether so-and-so has a drinking problem, or trashing so-and-so's kid who undeservedly made the A-team, or grumbling about the pastor's sermon that ran too long. She speaks with wisdom because she wisely considers her words before she opens her mouth. When in the presence of gossip or hearsay, the law of kindness remains on her tongue. With an awesome fear of the Lord, she is quick to remember "that men will have to give account on the day of judgment for every careless word they have spoken" (Matt. 12:36).

Her husband has full confidence in her and lacks nothing of value. She brings him good, not harm, all the days of her life.

PROVERBS 31:11–12

Define *Good*

Chapter 9 Perhaps one of the most intimidating challenges presented in the Proverbs 31 passage are the opening verses regarding the role of the virtuous woman as a wife. At first glance, bringing our husbands good and not harm may sound rather simple. Until of course we finish out the verse and discover that the Proverbs 31 woman did her man good *all the days of her life.* For the average man this would boil down to a few simple tasks: place the remote control within his reach, provide him with a well-balanced diet of meat and potatoes, and wear something other than his oversized T-shirts to bed.

Keep in mind that Proverbs 31 was intended to be the Cliff Notes for *How to Snag an Awesome Wife 101* for single men. Even so, whether we are married or single, the passage gives a wealth of wisdom regarding some basic principles for being a virtuous wife. It would be impossible to do this very important topic justice in just one chapter. Entire books have been written to aid women in the pursuit to be godly wives. That having been said, in this chapter we will examine the intent of the verses in the passage and look at a few other key verses that relate to being a godly wife. The basics we cover will pertain to a wife's role in building a healthy marriage. While a husband has equal responsibility to build a healthy marriage, we will not address his role in order to stay in keeping with the primary theme of this book.

Throughout my years of serving in ministry to women, my heart has been grieved over the number of women who are involved in unhappy marriages. Many have shared the frustration they feel carrying the marriage alone and the pain of living with a husband who is uncaring, uninvolved, and more like a roommate than a spouse. If this is your case, I commend you for picking up this book, which demonstrates your desire to be a godly wife in spite of ungodly circumstances. While your temptation in reading this chapter may be to wonder *When is it my turn to get my needs met?* be reminded that God is fully aware of your situation and saddened that your husband is not loving you as Christ loved the church (Eph. 5:25). If the thought of reaching out to your husband is difficult, pray specifically that your actions will be motivated as unto God. Though it is a high calling, a truly virtuous woman will seek to be a good wife regardless of whether her husband is seeking to be a good husband.

1. Earn His Trust

Her husband has full confidence in her.
(Prov. 31:11a)

I remember a time early in my marriage when my husband would occasionally sit me down for the purpose of going over the budget. Now before I go any further, I need to give you an idea of how diverse our backgrounds are when it comes to money. Keith grew up with two very frugal parents who operated on a tight budget and did not believe in frivolous spending. The guy grew up teething on a calculator, and his first word was "coupon." He probably even saved his allowance. As an adult, he is a mini-clone of his parents. I think you get the picture. Needless to say, analyzing the budget was on his list of favorite pastimes . . . until he met me.

I grew up in a home where most everything I wanted, I got. I got a car at sixteen, wrecked it, and got another. I headed to college with a rather generous monthly allowance, a gas card, and a credit card to be used in times of emergency. Somehow I still managed to run out of money before the end of the month and was forced to discover creative ways to survive. Long before grocery stores accepted credit cards (remember those days?) I would drive across town to gas stations with food marts in order to use my gas card for food and gas. At the time it never dawned on me that what I paid for a loaf of bread, chips, and lunchmeat at the gas station could buy a month's worth of food at the grocery store.

My father once questioned me about an expense that had showed up on my "emergency" credit card statement. He was concerned and wanted to know what sort of unfortunate emergency had occurred. I explained that I had been asked out to a fraternity party, and upon looking in my closet and discovering that I was lacking just the right outfit, I was forced to drive to the mall and make an "emergency" purchase. My father completely understood, we hung up, and I went back to eating my six-dollar bologna sandwich from the gas station.

When I met Keith, he sensed that we were on two different wavelengths when it came to budgets—he had one and I didn't. Regardless, we knew that our love for each other would enable us to overcome any silly little differences over money management. Hah!

I'm not sure when the initial sting of Cupid's arrow wore off, but I think it may have been the day he had to teach me how to pump my own gas. Once we were married, he was further appalled to discover that I had absolutely no idea how to balance a checkbook. When he asked me how I had survived in college, I told him that in order to come up with an accurate balance, I would fast from spending for three days in order to allow enough time for checks to clear and then get a reading of the balance at an ATM machine. I would then write that number in my checkbook, and voilà—checkbook was balanced! I was rather proud of myself for discovering this creative, time-saving method for balancing the checkbook, but he did not seem the least bit impressed. In fact, it seems I remember him saying in a rather sarcastic tone something to the effect of, "and you graduated with a degree in economics?"

So imagine how excited I was to attend these required early-in-the-marriage budget meetings. He would tediously go through the checkbook register and the bank statements and ask me to explain certain mystery purchases. I learned early on that he did not seem to be as lenient as my father had been with my so-called "emergency" expenditures. Never before had I been required to justify the need for multiple pairs of black shoes. It was sheer torture. My arguments of closed-toe versus open-toe, low heel versus medium heel, and dressy versus casual seemed to be lost on him. As I patiently attempted to justify the need for black strappy sandals and black calf-high boots, he mumbled something about one pair of black shoes being enough. Poor guy—had his mother not educated him to the natural link between a woman and her shoes? Maybe I should have worn the boots with my sundress to illustrate my point. It was no use, and as a result of my "frivolous" spending, I was put on a *budget*. The word became a curse word in my vocabulary.

Today we laugh when the word *budget* comes up in conversation. The grilling sessions over bank statements have ceased, and I have since earned his trust when it comes to money. Amazingly, we ended up meeting somewhere in the middle. I learned to tighten up and he learned to lighten up. I think I even convinced him of the need for multiple pairs of black shoes.

The Proverbs 31 woman's ability to go out and "buy a field" attests to the trust her husband must have had in her. In her culture it was very uncommon for women to initiate such large purchases. While I don't have my eye on any fields to buy (just give me *shoes!*), I have come to realize that finances are an area of importance to my husband. He has also come to realize that he can trust me not to break the bank because I have earned his trust over the years. *The Message* words verse 11 this way: "Her husband trusts her without reserve, and never has reason to regret it." In what areas does your husband trust you without reserve? Are there areas of importance where you may need to earn his trust? If you are not sure, ask him.

I love the following commentary about Proverbs 31:11: "She will be faithful. 'He shall have no need of spoil.' She will not be a spendthrift with her husband's money. She will be a helpmate or a helpmeet for him. God never intended woman to be a servant of man. She is to be his partner, and a real partner. When God made Eve to be a helpmeet, He made the other half of Adam. Adam was only half a man until God made Eve and gave her to him."[1]

2. Discover His Top Needs and Seek to Meet Them

. . . and lacks nothing of value. (Prov. 31:11b)

I remember a workshop I attended years ago at a women's conference that addressed meeting the needs of your husband. The speaker shared many worthy ideas that were sure to make my man a happy camper. I scribbled down the suggestions, all the while feeling a bit overwhelmed at the thought of implementing them all, especially with three small children clamoring to have their own needs met. After a week of knocking myself out to make him a homemade breakfast every morning, leaving a note in his lunch, organizing his socks by color, making our bed every day, staying on top of the chores, preparing dinner, and prettying myself up before he walked in the door, I was ready to scream "Calgon take me away" or better yet, take *him* away cuz this good-wifey business is harder than it looks.

Finally, we had a heart to heart and I shared that my deepest desire was to implement all these wonderful ideas so he would "lack nothing of value." Unfortunately, I was so exhausted from trying to pull it off that I ended up becoming bitter and cranky. Hardly the end result I had hoped for. To my relief, he informed me that while he greatly appreciated my sincere efforts, some of the things I was doing were not high on his list of needs. I was able to scratch through many of the items on the list, and in the end I discovered that, overall, he is a pretty simple guy. Make the bed—not important. Note in his lunch—thoughtful, but not necessary. Organize his sock drawer—focus instead on my lingerie drawer. If I could provide him with an occasional good meal, clean socks and underwear for a week's worth of work, happy children, and somehow manage not to fall into bed exhausted *every* evening, he'd be good to go in the needs department. Whew—mission accomplished.

In the first few months of our marriage, I was especially attentive to his needs. I was finishing my last semester of college and taking a light load of courses, so I had plenty of time to make him the center of my attention. I tried out new recipes on him and never missed his church league softball games. We joke today that I could have opened a pie shop that year. I think I spent more time in the kitchen in my first year of newlywed la-la land than all the other years combined.

Thirteen months later the pie shop closed with the birth of our first child. By our six-year anniversary, we had three kids ages five and under. The "chef's special" was chicken nuggets, macaroni and cheese, and apple juice. If he got a sudden sweet tooth, there was no shortage of graham crackers in the pantry. If the poor man got sick, his once attentive nurse was off the clock. Fortunately, his mom was a phone call away. The softball games I had once attended as his loyal fan became a source of bitterness and resentment as he sailed out the door for an evening of recreation and left me to do baths and bedtime stories alone. And that fancy lingerie I had received at my wedding showers—let's not even go there. If I had known what the first five years of my marriage would look like, I would have registered for sexy nursing gowns for my lingerie shower.

I'm sure I'm not the only wife who came out of the gates strong in meeting her husband's needs only to see it die down over the years. As I look back on it all, I'm not sure in all honesty that I could have done any better. It was all we could both do to keep our heads above water in our attempts to care for three small children. Keith was a real trooper and never expected me to do it all. In fact, as the insanity increased, we partnered together to do the laundry, get food on the table, and take care of the kids' never-ending list of needs. Was I attentive to his needs during that time? Not always. Was he attentive to my needs? Not always. Have we recovered? You bet! Our marriage has never been stronger, and as the kids have become more independent over the years, we have gained more time to focus on one another's needs.

During the early years, I would often beat myself up over the fact that I couldn't do it all. Finally, I candidly shared with my husband that I was frustrated that in the midst of caring for small children, his needs were often neglected. I told him that I sincerely desired to meet his needs more regularly, and I looked forward to a day when he could be the focus of my attention. If I had one thing I could do over in those early years with young children, I would have shared my frustration over not being able to meet his needs sooner. Just his knowing it was a desire of my heart seemed to strengthen our marriage.

Throughout my years of ministry to women, I have seen two contrasting mind-sets when it comes to the roles of husband and wife. This is important to discuss because it has a direct influence on a husband's *perceived* needs. There are some in the Christian community who sincerely

believe that a husband should never share in the housework or the care of the children. While this system may
work for some couples, it is not realistic for many dual-
income families. I cringe when I hear some in the
Christian community narrowly define the needs of men
and insist that deep down all men desire a *Leave It to
Beaver* setup in the home. While it is realistic that stay-at-
home mothers should assume the housework, today's generation of fathers desires to be involved in the care and
raising of the children. While this may be a foreign concept
to many in the older generation, the days of husbands
coming home from work and plopping into their easy
chairs to read the paper while their wives wrestle to get
dinner on the table, bathe the kids, and read them a bedtime story is considered a foreign concept to many in the
younger generation. The point is that we should be leery of
general quick-fix formulas to meet the average male needs.
The purpose of this chapter is to put aside the formulas
and help you discover *your* husband's primary needs so
you can then seek to meet them.

While I enjoyed those early years when my kids were
young (at least I think I did—it's all a blur), it was an
exhausting stage of life. Now that my kids can pack their
own lunches, do their homework without much assistance, stay home alone, and get this . . . I have one who can
even run errands for me, I am able to revisit some of my
husband's previous needs that went unmet in prior years.
It is like I came out of a fog and said, "OK, you look
vaguely familiar . . . tell me your name again." While our
lives are still busy, it's a different kind of busy. We have
more time for each other, and we are taking advantage of
it. We have even reached a point where we can look back
on those early years laughingly and say, "What was *that* all

about?!" While we have mixed emotions about our kids leaving the nest and the resulting unfamiliar silence that will permeate our home, we are also looking forward to the years when we can focus more on each other.

If you are in the stage of life where you have very small children who are not yet self-sufficient and you are feeling overwhelmed at the thought of focusing on your husband's needs, let me give you some basic rules to help lighten the load:

- Focus on your husband's primary needs (food, shelter, clothing, and um, sex).
- If you must omit something, then pick up fast food, leave the house a mess, postpone the wash, but concentrate on the last one—rare is the man who would prefer clean socks, a tidy house, or cooking in the kitchen more than cooking in the bedroom!
- Go on a date at least once every two weeks . . . alone—no kids!
- Don't talk about the kids on your date!
- Take a couple's trip or weekend getaway at least every couple of years.
- Smile more than you frown; laugh more than you cry.
- If you are a stay-at-home mom, don't neglect your appearance.

I realize that the last point is a sensitive topic. In my early years with young preschool children, my mentor, Ada, would remind me and the other young mothers in our Bible study group of the reality that our husbands are exposed to well-groomed, professional women on a daily basis at work. She cautioned us not to fall into the temptation to let ourselves go. Homemakers are sometimes stereotyped as frumpy, and I'm not so sure it is always without grounds. Many women seem to feel that once married, it is no longer necessary to wear makeup, fix their hair, dress up, or manage their weight, especially if they are hanging out with their kids during the day. I am certainly not saying that we have to look like super-models all the time, but let's be on guard that we don't let ourselves go. Whether you work or stay home, if your standard uniform is flannel jammie pants, no makeup, and a ball cap, trust me, he has noticed. It is possible to dress comfortably and still look attractive. Many husbands will be hesitant to say something, but rest assured, most every man desires that his wife be attentive to her appearance.

Somehow when I try to picture in my mind what the Proverbs 31 woman looked like, I imagine someone who could look polished and attractive whether she was in a corporate boardroom or doing the laundry. To let herself go would not be in keeping with her obvious commitment to doing everything with excellence. I can almost guarantee you that when her husband rose up and called her blessed, she wasn't sporting baggy sweatpants, slip-on loafers with white crew socks, no makeup, and a sloppy ponytail. When her husband shouted out her praises, he did so because she was attentive to all his needs. She was a picture of beauty both inside and out.

It makes sense that before we can ensure that our husbands lack nothing of value, we must first identify what they value. Each man is different, and what may be of value to one man may not be of value to another. Just as some men mistakenly assume that all women appreciate flowers and candy (just show me the money!), we would be wise to do our homework when it comes to our husband's needs. Make it a point to show him the verses in Proverbs 31, and ask him to share specifically what it is that would bring him value.

Although it is an uncomfortable topic for many women to talk about, there is no denying that most husbands would rank sex as a top need. I am burdened by the number of Christian women that view sex as a chore rather than a God-given expression of love for their spouse. Many confide that because they do not feel good about themselves, they find it difficult to believe they would be desirable to their husbands. True, men are visual creatures but trust me in this one—it doesn't take sexy size two lingerie to pull off a seduction. There is something very attractive about a woman who is comfortable in her own skin regardless of the readout on the scale. Tell your husband often that you desire him. E-mail him, call him, send him an instant message, or whisper it in his ear. And this one is a no-brainer—high waist granny panties and cross your heart bras have no place in a seduction. A little effort in the lingerie department goes a long way. Splurge and get something that makes you feel desirable.

My husband and I recently attended a mid-day award's assembly at our children's school. When we met in the parking lot to enter the school, he said, "Wow, you look nice." Honestly, my only motive that morning in getting dressed was to find something that didn't need ironing or scream "frumpy soccer mom." Apparently, it worked. We held hands during the assembly and when it was over, he walked me to my car. After he gave me a soft kiss good-bye, I said, "I'll see you later tonight," in a coy, flirtatious way that was loaded with a hundred different implications. Ladies, that's seduction. When I got home, there was an e-mail from my husband waiting in my inbox saying that he was having a hard time concentrating at work. Mission accomplished. If we are to meet our husbands' top needs we cannot ignore the fact that most men desperately desire to be desired. If you find it difficult to meet your husband's needs sexually, do something at once to remedy this problem. If necessary, see a counselor to get to the root of the issue. Your husband won't be the only one to reap the benefits.

Respect and Honor Him

She brings him good, not harm, all the days of her life. (Prov. 31:12)

I remember the first time I heard the phrase *high maintenance.* It was used casually among a group of men in reference to another man's wife. In addition to feeling uncomfortable over being an innocent bystander to forbidden gossip, I couldn't help but wonder what sort of deeds would earn a wife a place on the list of high-maintenance women. Did she run up the credit cards, hide the remote, or go out dancing after the kids were in bed? Would I make the list after years of dying Keith's T-shirts and underwear a pretty shade of pink? Regardless, I certainly didn't like the thought that someone might be buzzing on the grapevine about poor Keith Courtney and his high-maintenance wife!

Believe it or not, the Bible is chock-full of high-maintenance women. There are too many even to begin to name them all. Other verses allude to a possible high-maintenance characteristic when they speak of a "quarrelsome wife." Some compare her to a constant dripping on a rainy day (Prov. 19:13; 27:15), while others boldly state that it is better to live in a corner of the roof or in the desert than with a quarrelsome wife (Prov. 25:24; 21:19). Another verse says, "A wife of noble character is her husband's crown, but a disgraceful wife is like decay in his bones" (Prov. 12:4). Is there nothing in between— a crowning halo or rotting innards?

What exactly constitutes *quarrelsome*? Gone are the days where wives were to be seen and not heard and a wife's simple expression of her opinion in matters was considered quarrelsome behavior. Most men today desire a wife who is an equal partner when making decisions; they do not wish to carry the burden alone. However, as difficult as it is for many wives to accept, in situations where a mutual decision cannot be reached and a tie-breaker vote is required, Scripture indicates that a husband should hold the final vote as the head of the home.

The act of being quarrelsome relates to the attitude in which the wife conducts herself in regard to her husband. Is she a nagger? Is she difficult to please? Does she berate him with "I told you so" when he makes mistakes? Does she demean him in front of the children and others? Is her overall tone negative, condescending, and disrespectful? Once a decision is finalized, does she challenge his authority and question his judgment? Does she remind him of past failures?

Most Christian husbands today, mine included, would not consider it contentious or nagging for their wives to express their opinions and share in the decision-making process. If this is not the case in your marriage and your husband expects silent submission, you will need to take that into consideration, all the while praying that he will come to a proper understanding of the command in Ephesians 5:21 to "submit to one another out of reverence for Christ."

For the most part, the days when wives were expected to suppress their opinions and defer to their man in silent submission are over. Husbands who lord power over their wives and act more like domineering, rigid taskmasters than loving husbands are a dying breed. How very sad for the woman who must endure such a husband and even sadder should he attempt to justify his actions with a misunderstanding of the Ephesians 5:22 passage that instructs wives to submit to their husbands. Most godly men today are aware of the challenge for husbands to "love your wives, just as Christ loved the church and gave himself up for her" (Eph. 5:25). If one is to take the passage in context, it is clear that it was never the intent for husbands to treat their wives as doormats. Show me a marriage where the husband submits to God and seeks to love his wife as Christ loved the church, and I'll show you a wife who doesn't mind submitting to him. Whew! OK, enough said. Soapbox over.

Are You a Husband Basher?

Another area where wives have a tendency to do their husbands harm is by participating in the popular sport of husband-bashing. Most of us probably said words like *honor* and *respect* in our wedding vows, yet we tend to forget the meaning behind the words as time progresses and the love-is-blind and he-can-do-no-wrong phase comes to an end. For me, that phase ended the day we brought our firstborn home from the hospital and Keith left hours later for a softball tournament. The honeymoon was officially over. The Prince Charming I had married thirteen months prior was clearly on vacation. He did, however, beg my forgiveness when he got home (likely out of fear of being permanently banished to the couch for the remainder of our marriage).

However, in spite of his sincere repentance, it wasn't long before I found myself in a circle of girlfriends who were all too happy to share their husbands' most atrocious deeds in a public forum. Being the competitive person that I am, I couldn't resist the temptation to share the softball story, knowing it was worthy to take the prize. Even though my "he's such a cad" story easily trumped the others, I didn't feel like much of a winner. I felt an immediate pang of conviction over the disrespect I had shown my husband at the price of a laugh. It almost felt as if I had been disloyal to him and the vows we made to honor each other.

For the record, I have my husband's permission and blessing to share the infamous softball story in this book for the purpose of making a point. Husband-bashing happens so often it's predictable. In the quest to be virtuous women, we should avoid or, if need be, flee husband-bashing sessions. I cannot imagine many wives who would take kindly to their husbands sharing negative and often confidential information behind their backs to a circle of their best guy friends (not that it's realistic for them to get together and talk in the first place!). If caught, they would be sentenced to the couch for months.

Are You His No. 1 Fan?

Part of doing our husbands good and not harm, not to mention earning their trust, will be to speak highly of them, especially in the hearing of our children. Children should never be put in the uncomfortable situation of hearing Mom or Dad complain about the other. It breeds a sense of insecurity in the home if they witness their parents at odds rather than as a united front. Let them hear you brag on their father from time to time.

Perhaps one of the greatest needs among husbands is for their wives to be their No. 1 fan. I wonder how many successful men share the common denominator of a wife who is their constant cheerleader. And remember ladies, if they aren't getting the encouragement and support they need from us, they can always count on good ol' mom!— especially when they are sick and we simply respond to their list of "woe is me" symptoms by rolling our eyes. Of course, in my pursuit to be virtuous, I refrain and coddle him just as his mother would. There is no doubt that the Proverbs 31 woman had a positive outlook on life. I'm sure her husband was not perfect, but she likely chose to overlook his weaknesses and focus on his positive attributes.

As I consider the challenge presented in Proverbs 31:10–11, I am reminded of a marriage retreat where the speaker said something that I still think of often. He asked those of us in the audience how much training we had each gotten to help us in the quest to earn a living. That could include elementary and high school, college, trade schools, or on-the-job training. The leader then went around the room and asked for the number of years from each person. The relatively small gathering compiled a total of several hundred years of training for the purpose of making a living.

Our leader next asked how much training we had gotten to help us in the quest to have a successful marriage. The group greeted him with mostly blank looks. Some had been to a previous marriage retreat. Someone even asked about a psychology class. Our leader allowed us to include anything that might lend itself to building a healthy marriage. When the total was tallied, it came to a pitiful couple of years of training.

Finally the leader drove the point home with a question: "Which is harder, making a living or having a successful marriage?" (We're not *even* going to ask about parenting!) We quickly recognized that building a home is a far greater challenge than building a career. Just compare the divorce statistics in any given year to the unemployment statistics. The majority of people will manage to feed themselves and put a roof over their heads, while only half of all marriages will succeed.

Do you get the point our retreat leader was making? Why would we, many of whom come from broken and dysfunctional homes ourselves, think for a minute that we could build a healthy marriage by ourselves? Fortunately, God never intended for us to go it alone. It takes two people relying on God every step of the way to build a healthy marriage. A virtuous woman will do her husband good and not harm all the days of her life, regardless of whether her husband returns the favor, because she seeks to please God above all.

Rise Up, O Little Ones!

Chapter 10

I will never forget a priceless moment when my youngest child, Hayden, was about six years old. He climbed up in my lap for some snuggle time, and out of the blue he blurted, "Mom, you are my kinda woman." I'm pretty sure that would constitute as a modern-day equivalent of calling me "blessed." Of course, now the little lad is older and has an image to maintain. What mother doesn't dream of a day when her grown children in some form or fashion say, "Mom, you did a bang-up job—thanks"? I say "grown" children because I can't imagine many teenagers rising up and calling their moms blessed. Show me a teenager who is doing that, and I'll show you a mom who is withholding food. I'm lucky if I can get my teens to rise up, period, each morning. When our kids are young, they think mom hung the moon; by the time they reach the teen years, they think she's from the moon. If you are in this phase of life, be patient—we all know what happens when they have children of their own. We will hear the long-awaited words, "Mom, how in the world did you do it?" I even find myself wondering if my mom was really the dork I perceived her to be in my teen years. Amazingly, she morphed into a wise and rational person after I became a mother.

If the Proverbs 31 woman had published a step-by-step manual, *How to Raise Up Kids Who Rise Up and Call You Blessed*, it would no doubt be a best-seller. When it comes to the job title of "mother," we put a minimum of eighteen years into each child before we see a realistic indication of whether our efforts will bear fruit when they venture out of the nest. We must remember that the Proverbs 31 woman likely didn't hear the words of praise until she had invested years of blood, sweat, and tears into the rearing of her children. She had earned their praise, likely, as a result of the verses leading up to the tribute to her virtuosity.

We know that:

• "She gets up while it is still dark; she provides food for her family and portions for her servant girls" (v. 15). Whose working for whom here? Did she iron their clothes too?

• "When it snows, she has no fear for her household; for all of them are clothed in scarlet" (v. 21). Did I just hear an excuse to hit the malls and *shop*?

• "She speaks with wisdom, and faithful instruction is on her tongue" (v. 26). Are we to assume she maintained this calm demeanor when her preschooler buried her car keys in the sandbox at the playground? Didn't she occasionally blow it and scream the familiar, "Leave your sister alone!" loud enough for the neighbors to hear?

• "She . . . does not eat the bread of idleness" (v. 27b). Rats. I guess that rules out the soaps.

If there was one verse, however, that sums up the primary role as "mother," it is likely Proverbs 31:27a: "She watches over the affairs of her household." Whether we women work in an outside job full-time, stay home full-time, or find some mixture in between, we can still put other things above the priority of God and/or family. Many women work because they prioritize material goods, or they fear that being a stay-at-home mom lacks challenge and fulfillment. On the other hand, many women stay home with their children full-time, but they prioritize a neat, well-kept home or a list of social or church activities above the needs of their children. Regardless of your situation, the most important thing is to check in regularly with God and ask him what is best for your family. Every situation is different, but fortunately none are out of the reach of God's guidance and control. I have met many working women who are just as attentive to what is going on in their homes as many stay-at-home mothers. And I have met many stay-at-home mothers who are just as consumed with outside activities as some working women who are overly committed to their jobs. A mother is first and foremost a manager of the home. This does not necessarily mean that she carries the load of the housework alone, especially if she works during the day. Regardless of who does what chores, she will be the one to set the tone and mood of the home with her attitude and actions.

Our homes should be safe, secure, and emotionally healthy. They should be havens for family members—a place where they long to be after a weary day at school or work. They should be places where laughter is commonplace, grievances are forgiven, and hurts are comforted. When a mother watches over the affairs of her household, she is attentive to the physical, emotional, and spiritual needs of those in her charge. Just as she is called to extend her hands to the needy, her children are at the top of her list.

It is impossible to do the topic of motherhood justice in one chapter, and let me start by making a disclaimer. I am not an authority when it comes to parenting. I do not hold a degree in childhood development or any sort of formal training related to parenting. I am, however, a mother of three children who desperately desires to raise her children to love Christ more than life itself. My children are not perfect, but I can honestly say, I enjoy them. Our home is filled with laughter, and my relationship with each one is unique and special. My husband and I are devoted to raising them to be physically, emotionally, and spiritually healthy, but we know that this does not ensure that they will always cling fast to the path of God. We know plenty of godly parents who have poured every ounce of their being into the rearing of their children only to suffer the heartache of a prodigal who goes astray. As mothers, we can do our part, but there are no guarantees that it will produce the end result we desire. Ultimately, we must acknowledge that each child is a unique individual who will make his or her own choices—some good and some bad.

I do not espouse to a particular parenting program. I read books from time to time, and I have gleaned tidbits of wisdom from each one. Some were especially helpful in addressing certain phases of my children's growth. However, the best parenting book on the market is unmistakably the Bible. The book of Proverbs is especially rich in contrasting wisdom and folly, which will lay the groundwork when building a foundation of character in our children's lives. Christian books (including this one!) are meant to be accessories that enhance our regular time spent in God's Word—they are not meant to be a replacement. That having been said, let us look at several hats the virtuous woman must wear when it comes to looking well to the ways of her household and addressing the primary needs of her children.

Physical Provider

Watching over the affairs of our household is so much more than simply meeting our children's basic needs for food, shelter, and clothing. When my kids were young, I used to measure myself against other moms—you know, the ones who bleach their kid's socks and underwear, iron their clothes, *and* put them away. Try as I may, my good intentions would last a few days, and then I would revert back to my old system: throw the clean clothes in a giant pile on my bedroom floor and have them each sift through it, find their clothes, and put them away. Amazingly, my youngest could pull this off at age four. While it certainly would be a nice perk to have clean, folded clothes and a mother who puts them away, my children have had to go without this luxury. I no longer beat myself up over it, as it has taught them responsibility over the years. We can only accomplish so much in a day. Unfortunately, we mothers have a tendency to focus on the things we are not doing well rather than the things we are doing well.

I recently had an experience that years ago would have left me wallowing in a woe-is-me-I'm-such-a-bad-mother pity party. My youngest (there's your clue—this kind of thing doesn't happen with the firstborn) was due at the ball field for a baseball game, and I discovered that his baseball pants and shirt were still in the washer. (Do I get partial credit because they were at least clean?!) Anyway, we grabbed the uniform, jumped in the car, and headed for the ball field. I decided we had no choice but to take the lemons and make lemonade. I told my son to put his pants on and be glad that they were damp because it was 90-something degrees outside. I then had him roll down his window and hold on tight to his jersey as it flapped in the wind. We both laughed all the way to the ball field. I'm sure we were quite the sight to passersby. By the time we arrived at the ball field, his jersey was nearly dry, my child was happy, we had made a memory, and I was still on the good-mommy list. In the end, all the boys looked the same (except one was a little damp). I couldn't help but snicker to myself as I sat on the bleachers and wondered how many boys had pulled their neatly folded jerseys out of their dressers and missed out on all the fun.

As mothers, we must also be careful not to define watching over the ways of our households as a responsibility to provide our children with their long list of wants. Most of us tend to want to provide our children with the things we ourselves may not have received—piano lessons, sports teams, select teams, summer camps, cool clothes, the latest gadgets, nice vacations, a college education, and the list goes on. If we're not careful, we can go overboard and raise weary, exhausted kids who grow up with a sense of entitlement and who think busy is the normal pace of life.

As a physical provider to our children, we want to raise children who do not take their blessings for granted. We have succeeded if, in the end, they are more focused on wanting what they have than on having what they want.

Emotional Facilitator

In a recent conversation with a friend regarding the challenges of parenting, my friend said, "When it's all said and done, I just want my kids to grow up and be happy." I'm sure we can all echo her sentiments, but as Christians, we must distinguish the difference between the world's brand of "happy" and God's brand of "happy." While the world aims for happiness through success, prosperity, and material possessions, Christians should, instead, aim for *joy*.

Years ago in my weekly young mother's group led by my mentor, Ada, it was not unusual for the group to turn into a "whine" fest at times over never-ending piles of laundry, sick children, unappreciative husbands, and you-name-it. Of course, Ada, being the godly woman she is, would listen empathetically but challenge us to live by Colossians 3:23, which says: "Whatever you do, work at it with all your heart, as working for the Lord, not for men." She made it clear that joy is a choice. It is not dependent on circumstances but is rooted in the knowledge that we are loved beyond measure by God.

I would go home encouraged by her gentle reminder, possessing a renewed commitment to find joy in everything. When my kids spilled juice on my newly mopped floor, I would try singing "The Joy of the Lord Is My Strength" over and over to brainwash myself while cleaning up the mess. It usually worked—until they dumped cereal on the floor before I finished cleaning up the juice. By that point my joy had taken a hike, dragging the song with it. Yet as I practiced this truth over the years, I began to notice that my attitude gradually changed, and along with it, so did my kids' attitudes. Now this is not to say that I don't still enjoy a good whine from time to time, but it's more the exception than the rule.

If we are to have homes filled with joy, we must first model joy to our children. Like it or not, we are the emotional facilitators of the home. You've heard it said: "If Momma ain't happy, ain't nobody happy." Being a mother is the most difficult job I have ever had. It forced me to address my own weaknesses. It forced me to become responsible. It forced me to get over my own issues so I could address my children's issues. It forced me to come to the end of myself. Praise God for children! Of course, my poor firstborn child got to be the guinea pig as I experimented with this parenting thing while trying to juggle my own emotional insecurities. Poor Ryan has the double whammy—firstborn child of two firstborn parents. (In addition to setting aside money for his college education, we are throwing in a little extra for therapy.)

If we are to look well to the ways of our households, we need to provide them with homes where their feelings are validated and treated with care. This will be difficult to implement for those mothers who grew up in homes where emotions were taboo or altogether ignored. I'm sure we all desire to raise children who feel comfortable trusting us with their innermost thoughts, fears, and feelings, but sadly, few of us have learned to trust anyone with our own. Take it from someone who stuffed her feelings and adopted a "buck up little camper" attitude early in life—it's nearly impossible to address your children's feelings if you've built walls around your own. One of my greatest spiritual breakthroughs in my Christian walk came through a marriage course—called Intimate Encounters—offered by my local church. The course was based on the book by the same name authored by David and Teresa Ferguson.[1] My clue to run should have been the word *intimate*. I was so antifeelings that my husband and I had to go through it twice (thanks to me, we flunked the first time!). We eventually graduated and went on to lead marriage small groups in our church. We even led a "Parenting with Intimacy" group in our church that trained parents to implement the same principles with their children that they had learned in their marriage group.

In my "intimacy training" I learned valuable tools, such as asking my children, "How did that make you feel when such-and-such happened or so-and-so said that?" I learned the art of responding to my children's hurts with compassion rather than facts, logic, and reason. I learned that it was OK to go to my children and say, "I was wrong for such-and-such. I am so sorry. Will you forgive me?" I learned the importance of getting into *their* worlds versus spending time with them and expecting them to get into mine. I learned the importance of reminding my children that when they are hurting, their father and I do not desire that they hurt *alone*. We are available to hurt with them. When my daughter hit the teen years and became more resistant to verbally sharing her feelings, I began to e-mail her occasionally and ask her open-ended questions. She found it a much more comfortable method of communicating with me (and more humorous at times—especially when I would e-mail her from the next room!). It provided a creative means of staying in touch with her during a time when many girls pull away from their parents. However, before you try this with your fickle teenager, be warned that had her father and I not established the intimacy principles early in her growing up years, I'm not so sure she would have replied to my inquisitive e-mails! If upon reading this you come to the conclusion that you have lost touch with your older kids when it comes to communication, focus first on building the relationship. Have no other motive than that of spending time with them. Pray that they will eventually see you as a safe and trusted harbor to whom they can bring their hurts, frustrations, and fears.

Can you imagine if the majority of adults today had been raised with such healthy communication principles in place? If people were to learn healthy methods for sharing their feelings, such as the intimacy principles I had the privilege of learning, I have no doubt that addictions and other forms of escape would decline. The need for counseling would decrease. Cases of depression would be reduced. Marriages would be more stable. Divorce rates would decline. Families would be closer. Churches would be healthier. And God's people would be equipped to move forward and tend to the needs of others.

Spiritual Trainer

I have no greater joy than to hear that my children are walking in the truth. (3 John 4)

In Deuteronomy 6:1–9, God, through Moses, lays out the responsibility of parents to be the primary spiritual trainers of their children.

Hear, O Israel: The LORD our God, the LORD is one. Love the LORD your God with all your heart and with all your soul and with all your strength. These commandments that I give you today are to

be upon your hearts. Impress them on your chil-
dren. Talk about them when you sit at home and
when you walk along the road, when you lie down
and when you get up. Tie them as symbols on your
hands and bind them on your foreheads. Write
them on the doorframes of your houses and on
your gates. (vv. 4–9)

In my book *Your Girl: Raising a Godly Daughter in an Ungodly World,* I shared that God is much more concerned that our children receive proper training in his truths and principles than a coveted spot on the A-team, their name on the honor roll, or even a college degree. While these things are worthy, they should not be our primary focus.

It is more important than ever that parents be purposeful about the spiritual training of their children, given the current times. Our culture preaches a brand of moral relativism to our children through media, music, magazines, and public education. Moral relativism states that each person defines his or her own morality, and what may be wrong for one person, may be right for another. Many Christian kids have fallen prey to this lie because they have not been taught that God established an absolute standard for right and wrong, and he alone is truth. If they are not taught this critical truth, many will be swept up in the current of the tolerance movement and led to believe they must accept all behaviors.

It is not enough to take them to church, put them in Christian schools, and say bedtime prayers. As mothers appointed by God to raise his children in today's world, we must set forth with purpose and determination. We must have a clear understanding of God's truths in order to impress them on the hearts of our children. Impressing God's truths on our children involves teaching them with our words and showing them with our actions. In other words, we must practice what we preach and preach what we practice.

According to a Purdue University study that examined how parents influenced the religious beliefs of students ages eighteen to twenty-five, it is not enough for parents to model their beliefs to their children if they want them to adopt their religious beliefs. "Parents have to talk about those beliefs and share their thoughts with their child," according to Lynn Okagaki, who conducted the study.[2] The study revealed that children were more likely to adopt their parent's beliefs when they had a clear understanding of what their parents believed.[3]

We must talk about God's truths when we sit at home and when we walk along the road, when we lie down and when we get up. And we must do so in the hearing of our children. A mother's commitment to pass down God's truths to her children can literally have an impact on the souls of future grandchildren and great-grandchildren for generations to come.

In a chapter of *Your Girl,* I addressed the high calling of motherhood and shared one of the most beautiful accounts of maternal love found in Scripture. First Samuel 1:11–28 tells the story of Hannah, a woman who was barren for many years. Hannah cried out to God for a son and vowed to give him over to God should God comply by meeting her request. God blessed her with a son, Samuel, and true to her word, she cared for him until he was weaned. She then brought him to Eli, the priest, to live out the remainder of his childhood years at the temple.

After he was weaned, she took the boy with her,
young as he was, along with a three-year-old bull,
an ephah of flour and a skin of wine, and brought

*him to the house of the LORD at Shiloh. When they
had slaughtered the bull, they brought the boy to
Eli, and she said to him, "As surely as you live, my
lord, I am the woman who stood here beside you
praying to the LORD. I prayed for this child, and
the LORD has granted me what I asked of him. So
now I give him to the LORD. For his whole life he
will be given over to the LORD." And he worshiped
the LORD there.* (vv. 24–28)

What mother could take a child she had nursed at her
breast, swayed to sleep in her arms, and watched take his
first wobbly steps, and put him in the care of a stranger
for the remainder of his childhood years? Only a woman
desperately dependent on God. After turning Samuel over
to Eli, the priest, the next verse gives us great insight into
her walk with God:

*Then Hannah prayed and said: "My heart
rejoices in the LORD."* (1 Sam. 2:1)

I'd be curled up in a fetal position sobbing my eyes out,
but Hannah is rejoicing! Dear mothers, let us pay close heed
to Hannah's example. Our children belong first and foremost to the Lord. He has entrusted each of them into our
care for a short time. Even though Samuel was given over to
the Lord, he was not exempt from ungodly influences while
in the care of Eli. Scripture tells us that Eli's sons were guilty
of treating the Lord's offerings brought by the Israelites with
contempt and sleeping with the women who served at the
entrance of the Tent of Meeting. Ironically, it would be
Samuel who would eventually deliver the Lord's spoken
judgment against the house of Eli.

As my children get older and are exposed to ungodly
influences outside of my care and control, I have had to
mentally turn them over to the Lord as an act of my will.

I cannot watch them every minute of every day, but God can. Hannah was able to follow through with her vow to commit her son to the care of the Lord because she had come desperately to depend on God prior to Samuel's birth. When Hannah was barren, we are told that she poured out her soul to the Lord (1 Sam. 1:15). The original Hebrew word used for "pouring out" is *shaphak,* which means to "spill forth" or "sprawl out." Hannah was in the habit of depending on God long before she had children. Vow or no vow, Hannah knew better than to think Samuel belonged to her.

If we are to watch over the affairs of our households, we would be wise to acknowledge that our children belong first and foremost to God. He never intended that we wing this parenting thing alone. Whereas Hannah physically gave her child over to the Lord, we must mentally give our children over to the Lord. Hannah was in the habit of crying out to the Lord long before Samuel was born. There will be times when our children leave us no alternative but to cry out to the Lord and trust him for the results. We can rest assured that as concerned as we may be that our children walk with God, God is all the more concerned.

In the meantime, get to know your children. Talk to them. Spend time with them. Play with them. Laugh with them. Weep with them. Pray with them. Tell them often that you value them for who they are and not for what they do. Apologize to them when you blow it. Love your husband and speak highly of him. But most importantly, let your children witness that the most important thing in your life is your relationship with Jesus Christ. A mother's greatest calling is to pass on to her children the value of a deep and intimate relationship with Jesus

Christ. It's the gift that keeps on giving. While I can't guarantee you that watching over the affairs of your household will, in the end, produce children who rise up and call you blessed, rest assured—you have caught the eye of the Father. Nothing will compare to hearing him say, "Well done, my good and faithful servant."

The Defining Quality of the Virtuous Woman

Chapter 11	

When my daughter was in second grade, she was chosen to perform on an award-winning cheer squad for a fund-raising event. The practices were mandatory due to the fact that the absence of one person could affect the entire performance. She was the youngest member of the group, and the rest of the girls ranged in age from late elementary through high school.

One afternoon when I picked her up from practice, she was especially quiet on the way home. Sensing something was not right, I asked her if anything had happened during practice that had upset her. In response, she burst into tears and said that the song they were using in the performance said "something very bad" and that she was afraid that if she told me, I would pull her from the performance. Just days away from showtime, this clearly would not have settled well with her coach or the rest of the team. I asked her to tell me what part of the song had upset her. She continued to tell me that it was "really, really bad" and that she didn't want to say it out loud. Of course, by this time I had assumed the absolute worst and encouraged her that it would be OK to say it in this situation. Finally she leaned over and whispered, "Oh my God." Apparently the song had a part where the phrase was used in a sarcastic tone, thus upsetting my daughter.

The next day I shared the story with her coach. She was stunned that any child would put the phrase "Oh my God" on the same level as an offensive curse word. In the end, I decided to keep her in the performance based on the fact that pulling her out would have done more harm than good. I did however, let the coach know that we were opposed to songs in the future that showed irreverence to God. I was very proud of my daughter and commended her for responding to the lyrics with a tender "fear of the Lord" at the young age of seven. I prayed that she would continue to exhibit the same sensitivity to words that defame her Lord as she progressed in age and became more and more exposed to the improper use of God's name.

Fear of the Lord seems to be a forgotten practice in today's culture, even among the religious. While fear of God is emphasized more in the Old Testament and love of God is emphasized in the New Testament, it was never meant to be excused from our daily practice of worshipping God. In fact, Acts 9:31 reminds us that the early church "grew in numbers, living in the fear of the Lord." Regardless, many Christians are never taught what it is to fear God and, therefore, deem it to be unimportant. As women who desire to be virtuous, we cannot excuse this necessary attribute displayed by the Proverbs 31 woman.

In fact, if there is one verse that summarizes the sheer essence of who this woman was, it is Proverbs 31:30. The virtuous woman's ability to fear God was at the very core of her being. Without it, one could argue that it would be impossible to develop the other attributes spoken of in the passage. In fact, both Psalm 111:10 and Proverbs 9:10 clearly say that "the fear of the LORD is the beginning of wisdom."

Job also recognized the value that comes in fearing the Lord. He spoke of our human accomplishments and the ability to dig tunnels in the earth to make it give up its gold and precious stones. However, Job contrasts the miner's search with another. In 28:12 he asked where wisdom can be found. His comments accentuate how much greater this quest is. "Man does not comprehend [wisdom's] worth" (v. 13). "It cannot be bought with the finest gold, nor can its price be weighed in silver" (v. 15). "The price of wisdom is beyond rubies" (v. 18). At the end of his discourse, Job concludes that "the fear of the Lord—that is wisdom, and to shun evil is understanding" (v. 28).

The Proverbs 31 woman recognized that attainment of wisdom (discussed earlier in chap. 7), would not have been possible were it not for her ability first and foremost properly to fear God. The verses in Proverbs 31 that precede verse 30 almost appear to build up to one conclusive quality that summarizes virtue—fear of the Lord.

The Whole Duty of Man

King Solomon was someone who was known for possessing great wisdom. Though he personally had reaped the benefits of wealth, knowledge, and power, he continued to question the meaning of life. At the end of Ecclesiastes, he concludes the following:

> *Now all has been heard; here is the conclusion of the matter: Fear God and keep his commandments, for this is the whole duty of man.*
> (Eccl. 12:13)

We would be wise to accept that the fear of the Lord is our whole duty as well. The Proverbs 31 woman's ability to fear the Lord was a key factor in her being set apart from other women. If we are to become virtuous, we must possess this attribute. We must set out to discover what exactly it means to fear the Lord.

A Different Type of Fear

The Bible mentions several types of fear, so we need to understand the type of fear spoken of in the phrase "fear of the Lord." At first glance we might wonder if the fear of the Lord is the same type of fear we are most accustomed to experiencing, equated with being "afraid." Do we fear God the way some women have come to fear an angry or unpredictable mate? Do we fear God because he seeks to harm us?

The *Holman Bible Dictionary* describes secular fear as the natural feeling of alarm caused by the expectation of imminent danger, pain, or disaster; religious fear, on the other hand, appears as the result of awe and reverence toward a supreme power. It goes on to say that this sense of fear comes as individuals encounter the divine in the context of revelation. When God appears to a person, the person experiences the reality of God's holiness. This self-disclosure of God points to the vast distinction between humans and God, to the mysterious characteristic of God that at the same time attracts and repels. There is a mystery in divine holiness that causes individuals to become overwhelmed with a sense of awe and fear. The *Holman Bible Dictionary* further concludes that the fear of God is not to be understood as the dread that comes out of fear of punishment, but as the reverential regard and awe that comes out of recognition and submission to the divine. It is the revelation of God's will to which the believer submits in obedience.[1]

New Unger's Bible Dictionary describes fear of the Lord as something that

- dreads God's displeasure,
- desires God's favor,
- reveres God's holiness,
- submits cheerfully to God's will,
- is grateful for God's benefits,
- sincerely worships God, and
- conscientiously obeys God's commandments.[2]

It also states that fear and love must coexist in us before we can please and rightly serve God.[3] Apparently God knew we would need to learn godly fear before we would be able to know heavenly love. Hebrews 4:16 encourages us to approach God's throne of grace with confidence so we may receive mercy and find grace to help us in our time of need. Think of a time you needed grace—maybe you committed a sin so atrocious that you still feel uncomfortable at the thought of it. Now picture yourself approaching God's throne of grace. You have an appointment with the Kings of kings and Lord of lords. He is waiting for you. You begin to approach the Great Almighty. Do you walk? Do you run? Do you hang your head low and drag your feet? Once there, what do you say?

No doubt, most of us would be filled with awe and reverence (a healthy fear of the Lord) as we approach him. Would we also come with confidence and total assurance that our God is approachable and will not cast us away? Christians can take comfort in the fact that Jesus is our High Priest, so we can approach the throne of grace with confidence (Heb. 4:16). Loving and fearing God are inextricably linked. You could think of it this way: we cannot know God apart from faith in his Son, and we cannot fear God if we don't know him. Jesus said, "I have come that they may have life, and have it to the full" (John 10:10). Paradoxically, fearing the Lord is a critical aspect of having that abundant life. Would it surprise millions of ineffective, defeated, unhappy Christians to know that a key part of their problem is that they do not fear God?

Look over the list of characteristics that describe what it is to properly fear the Lord on pages 176–177 and ask yourself, on a scale of one to ten, how you would currently rate on each attribute. Consider making a note of any one (or more) in which you consider yourself to be deficient.

Fear of the Lord: A Biblical Account

If we seek a biblical example of what it is to fear the Lord, we must start in the Old Testament. Many people struggle with reconciling the God who showed wrath and judgment in the Old Testament with the God who sent his Son to die for mankind in the New Testament. At one point, this served as a barrier to my embracing the Christian faith. When I finally gave my life over to Christ, many of my questions remained unanswered, but I had come to a point where my need for forgiveness outweighed my need for answers. I knew that in time I would gain a better understanding of the God of the Old Testament.

Over the years I have gained a better understanding as a result of my commitment to read and study God's Word. While I had a basic understanding of what it was to fear the Lord, it wasn't until I read the account of the Israelite people and their exodus from Egypt that it came to life. There is perhaps no greater passage in Scripture that illustrates fear of the Lord than the Exodus account. So important was the concept of fearing the Lord that Moses, at the end of his life, devoted his final words to commanding the priests to read through the book of the law (Deuteronomy) every seven years in the hearing of the people. The purpose of this is given in Deuteronomy 31:12: "Assemble the people—men, women and children, and the aliens living in your towns—so they can listen and learn to fear the LORD your God and follow carefully all the words of this law."

The book of the law that Moses referred to was the Exodus account and the entrance into the Promised Land some forty years later. God knew that the Exodus account, if remembered and passed down from generation to generation, would provide the proper foundation for learning to fear the Lord. The command to read the account aloud every seven years ensured that the story would never die and that those who had failed to witness the account firsthand would have an opportunity to learn to fear the Lord by hearing the account. To share the account every seven years may seem like overkill, but good things bear repeating. It would be difficult to escape hearing the Exodus account if Moses' command was followed. Each generation, upon hearing the account every seven years, had an obligation to then pass the story to the next generation and so on and so on and so on.

If you are feeling overwhelmed with the realization that until now you have not had a proper understanding of what it is to fear the Lord, be assured that the same passage that was handed down by the Israelites from generation to generation can be your instructor as well.

The Exodus Account

> *Come, my children, listen to me; I will teach*
> *you the fear of the LORD.* (Ps. 34:11)

When the Exodus is properly understood, it becomes a love story second only to the sacrificial death of Christ. God kept his promise to his people when, after four hundred years of serving as slaves to the Egyptians, he raised up Moses to deliver them from Egypt and into the Promised Land. As we overview the Exodus account and the deliverance of the Israelite people, imagine that you are an Israelite. This will help you gain a better appreciation for the miracles that took place along the way.

The book of Genesis ends with the large family of Jacob living in Egypt. The decades turned to centuries, and the family of seventy became a great multitude in the land. As time passed, Joseph and his good deeds in Egypt were long forgotten. A new pharaoh arose who did not know of Joseph's past fame, and as a result, this new dynasty grew to hate and fear the Israelite people. Soon they began to institute plans to prevent the growth of the children of Israel. The Egyptians made slaves of the Israelites, forcing them into hard labor. Yet the more the people were oppressed, the more they increased in number.

> *Then a new king, who did not know about*
> *Joseph, came to power in Egypt. "Look," he said to*
> *his people, "the Israelites have become much too*
> *numerous for us. Come, we must deal shrewdly*
> *with them or they will become even more numer-*
> *ous and, if war breaks out, will join our enemies,*
> *fight against us and leave the country."*
> (Exod. 1:8–10)

To put a halt to this, the pharaoh ordered the Hebrew midwives to kill all the boys born to the Israelite women. The midwives, however, "feared God" more than the pharaoh and allowed the boys to live. Moses was one of the boys born during this time, and out of fear his mother placed him in a basket and floated the basket in the reeds along the banks of the Nile. When the pharaoh's daughter came to bathe in the river, she heard the cries of the infant and was touched. As a result, she decided to keep the boy and raise him in the palace as her own son. Little did she know that Moses' birth and her subsequent discovery of him were all part of a divine plan authored by God. As Moses grew up in the palace, his people were suffering as slaves and were used "ruthlessly" by the Egyptians (Exod. 1:14). Put yourself in the Israelites' place. How do you imagine they were feeling? Have you ever been used (ruthlessly) for another's personal gain? Did they view you as a person of worth or as a means to an end?

After years of being in bondage to the Egyptians, the Israelites finally cried out for deliverance to the only one who could help. Unbeknownst to them, God's plan of deliverance was already in place to free his people, and it would be implemented through Moses.

> *The LORD said, "I have indeed seen the misery*
> *of my people in Egypt. I have heard them crying*

> out because of their slave drivers, and I am con-
> cerned about their suffering." (Exod. 3:7)

Does this sound like a distant God who does not care for the sufferings of man? All along God had been working behind the scenes weaving the tapestry of his perfect plan. This plan of deliverance was revealed to Moses after he fled to Midian in an attempt to hide out after killing an Egyptian he had witnessed beating an Israelite. One day he was a fugitive on the run, and the next, a divinely appointed leader of approximately six million people. Moses, no doubt, experienced a healthy fear of the Lord as he stood before the burning bush that echoed God's divine plan of deliverance.

Following God's commands, Moses returned to Egypt and appeared before the pharaoh, boldly saying, "This is what the LORD, the God of Israel, says: 'Let my people go, so that they may hold a festival to me in the desert'" (Exod. 5:1).

Sounded simple, didn't it? But life seldom follows a simple script, and Pharaoh refused to let the people go. God reminded Moses of his promise, and Pharaoh's predicted hardness of heart. God already knew Pharaoh would refuse to allow the people to go until a series of plagues devastated the land. Before the plagues began, Moses was given the difficult task of convincing the Israelite leaders of God's plan for deliverance. The Israelite people were not immediately convinced of God's plan, and at one point blamed Moses and Aaron for the increase in their workload after they had unsuccessfully appealed to Pharaoh to let the people go and worship. Consider how the plagues demonstrated not only God's awesome power to Pharaoh but also served to further convince the Israelites of his love for them in order that they might trust and follow Moses. If you were an Israelite living during this time (trust me, you *don't* want to be an Egyptian in this drama!), at what point in the game would you begin to fear God (awe and revere him)? Read through the following summary of plagues and determine what it would take for you to drop to your knees in reverence to an almighty God who had gone to great lengths to free you from your oppression.

The Plagues: Ten Opportunities to Fear the Lord

Plague 1: God turns the waters of the Nile to blood. No doubt, it was the talk of the town. The Egyptians depended on the life-sustaining waters of the Nile. Some theologians believe God may have had a dual purpose in turning the waters to blood in order to represent the innocent blood of the Hebrew newborn boys whom Pharaoh had ordered thrown into the Nile. It's hard to imagine any other explanation of such an occurrence other than the mighty hand of God, but as with most things, there are always doubters in every bunch. Would you have been one of them?

Plague 2: Vast hordes of frogs invade. Frogs came up from the river and infested every home in Egypt. They were found in the beds, ovens, and kneading bowls. When God ordered an end to the plague, they were piled up in heaps, and the land reeked with their stench. In Egypt, frogs were the symbol of fertility. Could this be a mockery of Pharaoh's failed attempts to limit the population of the Israelites?

Plague 3: Gnats infest the land. The dust of Egypt was transformed into gnats. Gnats basically means lice or stinging gnats. Pharaoh's magicians could not duplicate this plague and advised Pharaoh that this plague was most surely the finger of God. As predicted, Pharaoh's heart grew harder.

Plague 4: Flies swarm the land. Flies filled every home and covered the ground. It is said that the entire land was thrown into chaos by the flies. This plague was exclusive to the Egyptians and did not affect the Israelites' land. God made this distinction to show his favor to the Israelite people.

Plague 5: Deadly plague kills the livestock. This plague was exclusive to the livestock of the Egyptians and killed off many of their horses, donkey, camels, cattle, sheep, and goats. The livestock of the Israelites remained untouched to further show God's favor to the Israelite people.

Plague 6: Boils infect the Egyptians. Moses tossed soot into the air and terrible boils broke out on the Egyptians and their animals. Pharaoh's magicians, who had been able to duplicate a few of the initial plagues, also broke out in the boils and were powerless at the hand of God.

Plague 7: God sends a hailstorm worse than any other in Egypt's history. God warned Pharaoh through Moses that he could have wiped them all from the face of the earth by now but that he allowed them to live that they might see his power and his fame might spread throughout the earth. Moses warned Pharaoh that any man or beast left outside would be killed by this storm. Exodus 9:20 says, "Those officials of Pharaoh who feared the word of the LORD hurried to bring their slaves and their livestock inside." In spite of the Egyptians' strong belief in gods and goddesses, many were beginning to "fear" the Lord.

Plague 8: God covers the land of Egypt from border to border with locusts. What few crops had survived the hailstorm were now destroyed by the locusts. So many covered the ground that it was black, and when they were finished, not one green thing remained. Scripture says there had never been locusts such as these, nor shall there be in the future.

Plague 9: Darkness covers the land for three days. A deep darkness fell over the land of the Egyptians only, but the Israelites continued to have light in their dwellings. Where was the revered Egyptian deity, the sun god Ra, during this plague?

Plague 10: Death of the firstborn of every family and animal. The last plague was the most devastating to the Egyptians and included the death of all the firstborn in the land of Egypt, from the firstborn of Pharaoh to the firstborn of livestock. There was a great cry in the land of Egypt, for there was not a house where there was not one dead.

God had given the Israelites specific instructions on how to ensure that they would be spared from losing their firstborn to the plague of death. By sacrificing a lamb and putting its blood on the sides and top of their doorposts, the angel of death would know they belonged to the Lord and would pass over them. Thus it is remembered as the Passover. The Israelites were told that the Passover should serve as a day to commemorate and celebrate for generations to come. It serves as a reminder of God's love and mercy in delivering the Israelites out of Egypt.

True to God's word, Pharaoh allowed the people to go after suffering the loss of his own son. The exodus from Egypt began with an estimated two million Israelite men and their respective families leaving Egypt (approximately six million people) with their livestock, unleavened dough for making bread, and materials handed over by the Egyptians. As predicted by the Lord, they also plundered the Egyptians.

Stop for a minute and imagine the scene. The Israelites had been slaves for much longer than anyone living could remember. Now, after the ten plagues, they find themselves leaving Egypt carrying much wealth in gold and silver jewelry. As they left the only place they had ever known, the land was virtually unrecognizable. The plagues had left it a vast wasteland. God's power was evident everywhere they looked. As they joined the never-ending procession of people leaving Egypt, how do you suppose they felt? I think it is safe to assume that they were experiencing an awesome fear of the Lord.

Even for the Israelites who did not experience the Exodus firsthand but rather heard about it many years later as a result of the required reading of the book of the law every seven years, it would be unusual to be left with any emotion other than a deep fear of the Lord. And to think that the journey was only beginning. There were many more opportunities in the wilderness for God to display his power and might.

How about you? Would you have been a first-plague believer, a second-plague believer, or would it have taken nine plagues to convince you of God's presence and power? Clearly, all of the Israelites had signed on to the plan by plague 10 (I can assure you that not one was sitting in their home contemplating whether to follow Moses' instructions regarding the slaughter of the lamb and wiping its blood on the sides and top of the doorframe of their home). What would you be feeling toward God as you exit Egypt? Do you believe that the God who performed these miracles is the same God that you believe in today? If so, does he still deserve to be awed and revered?

Fear of the Lord Turns to Fear

The Israelites surely felt awe and reverence toward God for the great miracles they had witnessed. He had delivered them from an increasingly painful situation as slaves. Yet just days into their exodus from Egypt, they must have been shocked to hear the thundering of horse's hooves and to look back to see the Egyptian army coming after them in hot pursuit. Pharaoh had changed his mind—he decided to make one last attempt to prevent them from leaving by hemming the Israelites in at the Red Sea.

Exodus 14:10 tells us that the situation brought two very different responses from the Israelite people. First they were terrified. Hardly a response of faith. Before you come to their defense, be reminded that in addition to the ten plagues, God had further aided them in their escape after the final plague. He had sent a pillar of cloud to guide them by day and a pillar of fire to guide them by night. They had no reason to fear as they witnessed the presence of God before them. The Israelite's second response was better. In their terror, they cried out to the Lord.

It's almost humorous when you consider that their statement to Moses, "Was it because there were no graves in Egypt that you brought us to the desert to die?" (Exod. 14:11), was made with the God of the universe before them and the army of Pharaoh behind them. Talk about slow learners! It's a wonder God didn't zap them dead for their unbelief.

In all honesty, what would your response have been? Understandably, it would be a bit unnerving to hear the thundering sound of horses' hooves closing in behind you. Yet wouldn't you have grown accustomed to expecting another miracle by this time, fresh on the heels of being spared from ten miraculous plagues? Would you pull a Dorothy and tap your slippers together and chant, "There's no place like home"? Would you gather your little munchkins together and scribble out your last will and testament on a piece of tree bark? I don't know about you, but I'd like to think I'd grab the kids, face the Red Sea, and say, "Watch this, kids! God is about to wow us again with another display of his mighty power!" Yet, if we are honest, I wonder if we would have responded any differently from the Israelites that day. One minute they were filled with unspeakable awe and reverence toward God, and the next minute they were whining like a bunch of babies.

Should they have been surprised that God had yet another plan and was once again using the situation to display his power? Sure enough, when Moses raised his staff, God parted the Red Sea. To protect the Israelites from the approaching army, an angel of God withdrew from the front and went behind them. The pillar of cloud also moved behind the Israelites and brought darkness between them and the Egyptians. The waters of the Red Sea rose up on either side so that the Israelites could cross over. As the Israelites walked through, the Egyptians pursued them. The pillar of cloud threw them into confusion; their chariot wheels fell off. Once the Israelites reached the other side, Moses again raised his staff, and the water swept over the Egyptian army. Not one of them survived.

Exodus 14:31 tells us: "When the Israelites saw the great power the LORD displayed against the Egyptians, the people feared the LORD and put their trust in him and in Moses his servant." Did you catch that? Fear of the Lord leads to *trust*.

I imagine some of them even felt a little silly that they had wasted even one second experiencing freak-out mode.

I find it somewhat amusing that after witnessing so many miracles prior to the Exodus, the Israelites suddenly assumed the Great Miracle Maker was on his lunch break. Throughout their journey in the wilderness, the Israelites would witness many more miracles. Unfortunately, the Israelites' awe and reverence of God always had a short life-span, and truth be told, I'm afraid we're probably no different.

Again and again throughout the forty years of wandering in the wilderness, we see the same pattern among the Israelite people. God would display his power, and the people would fear him—for a time. Once their initial awe wore off, they would rebel again and sin. God would become angry. Moses would intercede on behalf of the people, and as a result, God would spare them. Even after their ridiculous incident with the golden calf and their gall to proclaim it the god who brought them up out of Egypt (Exod. 32:4), God forgave them. And this was only one of many incidences where their fear of the Lord was replaced with rebellion.

However, their sin was not without consequences. As a result of their failure consistently to fear the Lord, all of the men twenty years or older would die in the desert. Only their children would enter the Promised Land. After all they had witnessed leading up to the Exodus and all the time they had wandered in the wilderness, you would think they would have this "fear of the Lord" thing down by now. What a price to pay. Only two men were exempt from the consequences: Joshua and Caleb.

What was it about Caleb and Joshua that set them apart from the others? After scouting out the Promised

Land with others and discovering that it was inhabited and would require a battle before it could be occupied, they never doubted that it was part of God's plan. They trusted God to the very end. The others reported back to Moses, grumbling with doubt that the battle could be won and stirring up dissension among the people. They even spoke of appointing a new leader who would take them back to Egypt! In Numbers 14:7–8, Joshua and Caleb say to the community of Israel: "The land we explored is a wonderful land! And if the LORD is pleased with us, he will bring us safely into that land and give it to us. It is a rich land flowing with milk and honey, and he will give it to us!" (NLT).

Throughout the wilderness experience, God points out to Moses how quickly the people forgot his mighty works and failed to remember their deliverance at his hand. It seems to me that the ability to remember what the Lord has done in our own deliverance at the Lord's hand is the key to consistently fearing the Lord as Joshua and Caleb demonstrated. They never forgot what they had witnessed, and neither should we.

Self-check: If you had been among the Israelites who made the exodus from Egypt, would you have been known more for your incessant grumbling or for your consistent fear of the Lord? Like the Israelites' deliverance from Egypt, how have you been *delivered* by God? I hope you are able to connect the beautiful symbolism of the Old Testament deliverance of the Israelite people to the deliverance God offers today through his Son's death on the cross. Are you in the habit of remembering it? That alone is worth a lifetime devoted to fearing the Lord. Pray and ask God to give you the ability, with the help of the Holy Spirit, to follow him wholeheartedly in the days to come.

> He gave them these orders: "You must serve
> faithfully and wholeheartedly in the fear of the
> LORD." (2 Chron. 19:9)

Out of all of the Israelites who were part of the
Exodus, only Caleb and Joshua were allowed to enter
the Promised Land (Num. 14:30). One can safely assume
they were chosen because they had served "faithfully
and wholeheartedly in the fear of the Lord." Another
beautiful passage of Scripture that speaks of a select few
who fear the Lord is in Malachi 3:16–18:

> Then those who feared the LORD talked with
> each other, and the LORD listened and heard.
> A scroll of remembrance was written in his pres-
> ence concerning those who feared the LORD and
> honored his name.
>
> "They will be mine," says the LORD Almighty,
> "in the day when I make up my treasured posses-
> sion. I will spare them, just as in compassion a
> man spares his son who serves him. And you will
> again see the distinction between the righteous
> and the wicked, between those who serve God and
> those who do not."

Would You Make the List?

Though it does not come anywhere close to comparison, I still remember the excitement I felt when I was
elected as one of six cheerleaders out of more than one
hundred girls trying out in junior high school. Like Caleb
and Joshua, I was selected as one of many, but that is
where the comparison stops. I was not selected for my
notable character but rather for my ability to do back
handsprings across the gym floor during tryouts. I will

never forget the pure elation I felt when I heard my name called over the public address system. I was chosen. I was something. I was one of a few girls who would get to don that uniform the following year. Are you impressed? I hope not!

Think of a time where you were chosen for something. What were you feeling at that time? Now imagine how it would feel to be recognized by God for your ability to serve faithfully and wholeheartedly in the fear of the Lord. How I would trade my name on that silly list of cheerleaders to have it listed on the Lord's scroll of remembrance as one of few who feared him and honored his name! That's the list I want to find my name on in the end. I would like to come to a point in my life where, more often than not, I can lay my head down to rest at night and tell God, "Today I have served you faithfully with all my heart. Nothing hindered me from doing your will."

> *Now, O Israel, what does the LORD your God*
> *ask of you but to fear the LORD your God, to walk*
> *in all his ways, to love him, to serve the LORD your*
> *God with all your heart and with all your soul,*
> *and to observe the LORD's commands and decrees*
> *that I am giving you today for your own good?*
> (Deut. 10:12–13)

Scripture abounds with benefits promised to those who fear the Lord. Ironically, many are the same benefits the world pursues. To those who seek longevity, God says, "The fear of the LORD is a fountain of life, turning a man from the snares of death" (Prov. 14:27). When it comes to the search for contentment, keep in mind that "happy are those who fear the LORD. Yes, happy are those who delight in doing what he commands" (Ps. 112:1 NLT) and "The fear of the LORD leads to life: Then one rests content, untouched by trouble" (Prov. 19:23). For those in search of true riches, "Humility and the fear of the LORD bring wealth and honor and life" (Prov. 22:4). And these are only a few of the many benefits that can come to those who fear the Lord.

I am deeply troubled by the number of people, Christians included, who have little, if any, fear of the Lord. Most people never give God the time of day. Few recognize him as the very Creator of life, and many of the few who do will never take the time to say thank you. The majority will pay homage to those who impress the world with their talents and skills, while ignoring the handiwork of God all around them. We are no different today from the Israelite people who quickly forgot God's covenant and pledge of unfailing love and turned their hearts to idols. God desires our whole heart. The Proverbs 31 woman followed God with a wholehearted devotion. If we desire to be virtuous women, we must be willing to do the same.

I fear God, and next to God I chiefly fear him
who fears Him not. (Saadi, a Persian poet)

The Proverbs 31 woman clearly had learned to fear the Lord and, as a result, served him faithfully and whole-heartedly. No doubt, she had been set apart, and Proverbs 31:29 records her legacy that "many women do noble things, but you surpass them all." Let us follow her godly example and grow in the knowledge and fear of the Lord. If we should leave this planet through the avenue of death, let's leave a legacy as women who served faithfully and wholeheartedly in the fear of the Lord.

*Give her the reward she has earned,
and let her works bring her
praise at the city gate.*

PROVERBS 31:31

The Gift That Keeps On Giving

Chapter 12 Mark Twain described a scene we all might secretly envy a bit. The townsfolk counted Tom Sawyer and his two friends as dead, so the trio got the opportunity to attend their own funeral service. They listened as the mourners proclaimed their affection and extolled the virtues of the deceased.

Imagine viewing your own funeral. You are sitting undetected in the back of the room as friends and loved ones come up one by one to say a few words about your life. Your husband, children, grandchildren, pastor, coworker, and neighbor summarize in paragraphs what your life was all about. What will they say? Will you be remembered for your contributions in the workforce? Will you be remembered for donating money to worthy causes? Will you be remembered as a friend to the friendless? Will you be remembered for your tireless devotion to the local church?

Your entire life has pointed to this very moment, and before your eyes your legacy begins to unfold. Qualities you possessed on earth will be molded into stories and memories and handed down to future generations. Your entire existence will be summed up with words describing who you were as a person, what you accomplished, and the legacy you leave behind. You begin to weep as you realize that your life is but a small speck on the time line of eternity. Do you weep with tears of joy or regret as this truth begins to sink in? Would you do things differently if given another chance?

Fortunately, it's not too late. Now is the time to think about the legacy you will someday leave. Who you are today will impact who you are tomorrow. What kind of statements would you someday hope your husband, children, friends, coworkers, or your pastor say? And are you becoming that kind of person? Are you in pursuit of developing qualities that will someday mold a legacy you can be proud of, or will you later realize that worldly success was the wrong goal to pursue? Are you chasing God's goals for your life, or like all of us at times, are you allowing circumstances to toss your life around, making your decisions for you?

When it comes to leaving a legacy, the Proverbs 31 woman certainly succeeded, especially given the fact we are still talking about this woman today. Even though she may, in fact, have been more of an ideal than real, we cannot ignore the tribute that comes to this virtuous woman. Aside from her children arising and calling her blessed and her husband praising her, her works themselves bring her praise at the city gate. This offers the hope that a woman who is intentional about being virtuous and living a life of purpose will no doubt leave a positive legacy for generations to come.

In 1 Corinthians 9:24–27, Paul reminds us of the futility of running for the world's prizes, which have only temporal, earthly value. We are challenged, instead, to run for a crown that will last forever. In the quest to leave a legacy as virtuous women, we should take heed of Paul's warning to avoid "running aimlessly" (v. 26). We won't leave a lasting legacy by happenstance. It will take commitment, hard work, and effort. Just as we might develop a plan to accomplish certain goals, this pursuit to be virtuous women is no different. Unfortunately, most Christians are no different from the rest of the world. Our tendency is to focus on the here and now rather than plan for the long-term future. If we are to run with purpose in this race called life, we must take the time to renew our minds with several truths that, unless understood properly, can lead to aimless running.

Truth 1: The Race Is a Marathon, Not a Sprint

I ran across the following statement that challenges me to intentional living: "You are who you've been becoming." That statement may comfort or disturb you, depending on your priorities. You will only get one chance at this life—this is not a dress rehearsal. Believe it or not, the legacy you leave behind can impact your family's lineage for generations to come. For most of us, it's enough of a challenge to live in the present, much less take thought of the "eternal" future. In a pleasure-seeking world that stresses instant gratification, most give little thought to developing qualities that will impact our own future, much less future generations.

I realize that the concepts discussed in this book are a tremendous challenge to many. Writing this book has been a humbling and often convicting experience for me personally. It has brought into the light many areas in which I need to improve. It would be easy to become overwhelmed with the whole pursuit. I like instant results, and often, in my zeal to change, I will put unrealistic expectations on myself. In the end I am often left discouraged and tempted to give up the whole pursuit.

In the quest to be a virtuous woman, I have had to remind myself along the way that it is a lifelong pursuit. Though my heart is sincere in the quest and desperately desires to see change, I won't wake up suddenly "virtuous" one morning. Part of running with purpose is learning to run the race at God's pace. We must see the pursuit not as a quick sprint but as a long-distance run.

I am reminded of a magnet I saw on a friend's refrigerator that said, "Be patient, He's not finished with me yet." No doubt it was inspired by Paul's encouragement to the Christians at Philippi: "He [God] who began a good work in you will carry it on to completion until the day of Christ Jesus" (Phil. 1:6). How promising that God is constantly refining us to be more like his Son. Hide that truth in your heart if you, too, are feeling overwhelmed with the pursuit to be a virtuous woman. If you struggle with perfectionism, be warned: this pursuit will drive you batty. Remind yourself that the Proverbs 31 woman appeared perfect because she was *make-believe*. With the same marvel that a small child displays at the thought of Santa Claus visiting every home in the world in one evening, we too should question the ability of one woman to be so perfect. As we measure ourselves against the qualities of the Proverbs 31 woman, we must remember that she was an *ideal*, not *for real!*

Our goals in this pursuit must be reasonable, or we will be tempted to give up along the way. I challenge you to go before God and ask him to narrow it down to three areas where you need improvement. Make a list of those three areas and then ask him to identify the one that needs immediate attention. Develop some tangible goals that will help you improve in that one area. If necessary, find an accountability partner who will ask you (lovingly) on a regular basis how you are doing in that one area. Once you have improved in that one area, move on to another one. We have our entire lives to work on our weaknesses, and God would never expect us to tackle them all at once. He will not give us more than we can bear.

Most importantly, when running this marathon, take the time to stop and catch your breath along the way. Be still before God and bathe yourself daily in his grace. As you stop and reflect on his unfailing love, it will give you the fuel and energy needed to run the next leg of the race. At times you may jog off course for a lap or two and become discouraged. If you find yourself off course, hold your head up high and jump right back in. In this race, the victories come when we focus on one leg of the race at a time. There will be small victories along the way when there is marked improvement in previous areas of weakness. The ultimate victory won't come until we cross the finish line.

Truth 2: We Do Not Run the Race Alone

If I had to pinpoint one reason why so many Christians continue running for worldly prizes when they should know better, I would say it boils down to the issue of dying to sin and self. Many Christian women are enticed by the world and give in to its desires. If we do not fully embrace the message of the cross, only time separates us from returning to the familiar and comfortable. Dying to sin and self is not a one-time event. It must be a daily (or for many, myself included, a moment-by-moment) exercise.

After I spoke on temptation at a women's event, a woman approached me. She had been a Christian for many years. She and her husband were very involved in their local church, and she taught Sunday school. They were committed to raising their four children in the church and to teaching them Christian principles. Then she dropped the bomb. She was having an affair with a coworker. It had been going on for more than two years, and a few times she ended it, only to resume it days later. She spoke confidently of her salvation and was more than knowledgeable when it came to God's forgiveness. She said she knew what she was doing was wrong, yet she seemed unwilling to give it up. She said that this man truly loved her and that he complimented her more than her husband. It felt too good to give it up. Because of that, she refused to die to this one area of sin and now, it was eating her lunch. She could not comprehend that obedience to Christ, though it meant dying to her desire to "feel good" in this man's presence, could actually *feel* better in the end. The enemy had done a number on her, and in her desperation to cling to this momentary pleasure, she was empty and miserable.

Her story brought to mind an episode involving my youngest son, Hayden, when he was five years old. He had caught a lizard and taken it to school for show-and-tell. When he got home that day, I encouraged him to let the lizard go free because it wasn't moving around much and I feared the worst. He had a friend over and they went outside to grant the lizard its freedom. Shortly, they came back with a flat rock and a permanent marker. (A permanent marker in the hands of a five-year-old is sure to get a mother's attention.) They explained that they had buried the lizard. The rock was to be the tombstone, and I was asked to assist them in writing an appropriate epitaph. Before helping them spell "This is my dead lizard" (Hayden's poetic creation), I asked them if the lizard had actually died. Hayden responded very matter-of-factly: "Mom, he was *almost* dead." The story has a happy ending. We were able to rescue the poor lizard in time. Amazingly, it appears the little fellow had been "playing dead" all along. When we uncovered him, he raced off with lightning speed. The funeral was canceled, and I doubt we will see him again.

> *In the same way, count yourselves dead to sin*
> *but alive to God in Christ Jesus.* (Rom. 6:11)

When it comes to sin, you can only play dead for so long before it catches up to you. If you're not careful, you could find yourself buried alive, like our lizard friend *and* the woman involved in the sin of adultery in the story above. It occurs to me that quite a few "almost-dead" Christians populate the world. Many attend Bible studies and serve in ministry leadership positions. They are knowledgeable about prayer and quiet times; they fill our church pews. Yet many refuse to fully die to certain areas of sin that they have allowed to master them. As a result, they are left with lives that are anything but *abundant.*

I think almost-dead Christians must be the most miserable people in the world because they battle a constant, unsettled peace that something better is out there. They know deep in their hearts that no earthly pleasure can compare to a deeper relationship with Jesus Christ, but in their stubbornness they refuse to give it up. One can only imagine the number of Christians with tremendous potential who have succumbed to the "feel-good" enticements of worldly pleasures and have forfeited the abundant life. Ironically, nothing feels as good as choosing God's ways over the ways of the world.

I certainly don't want to imply that dying to self is an easy task. Paul speaks of the paradox of doing the very thing you do not wish to do in Romans 7:14–25. *The Message* communicates Paul's battle with dying to sin in a way to which I think we can all relate:

> *I decide to do good, but I don't really do it; I decide not to do bad, but then I do it anyway. My decisions, such as they are, don't result in actions. Something has gone wrong deep within me and gets the better of me every time. It happens so regularly that it's predictable. The moment I decide to do good, sin is there to trip me up. I truly delight in God's commands, but it's pretty obvious that not all of me joins in that delight. Parts of me covertly rebel, and just when I least expect it, they take charge. I've tried everything and nothing helps. I'm at the end of my rope. Is there no one who can do anything for me? Isn't that the real question?* (Rom. 7:19–24 *The Message*)

Fortunately, in answer to his question, yes, there is someone who can help. I am comforted in the truth that we do not run this race alone. God has given us power through the Holy Spirit to combat every sin that will cross our path. It will be up to us to utilize that power. If we have not determined early on in the race that we run with God and for God, sin will not be far. Once we determine that the race is not about us, it will be easier to die to sin and self on a consistent basis.

Truth 3: We Run the Race for Eternal Prizes

Even though it was long ago, I can still remember sitting in the bleachers in my high school gym at the end of my senior year for the year-end awards ceremony. Having tied my worth to performance and peer acceptance, I had been purposeful over the years in acquiring many worldly titles. Unfortunately, while sitting in the bleachers listening to what seemed like every name in my senior class called out but mine, I experienced the sober realization that, perhaps, I had not put my efforts into the right activities, or at least the ones esteemed by faculty or the colleges. For someone who cared deeply about what others thought, awards day would have been the crowning moment of glory. Yet those who seemed to rake in the awards were virtually unknown in my peer group. Some would walk up to accept their award or scholarship only to have their name called out again before they could ever take their seat. *How ironic,* I recall thinking, *all these years spent investing in "popularity" and here I sit clapping for people I don't even know!*

I wonder if many Christians won't experience a similar conflict of emotions on the big awards day in heaven. Oh, there's no way to be sure what the ceremony will be like, but Scripture most assuredly speaks of rewards and crowns.

> *For we must all appear before the judgment*
> *seat of Christ, that each one may receive what is*
> *due him for the things done while in the body,*
> *whether good or bad.* (2 Cor. 5:10)

Although, as Christians, our salvation is secure, our deeds on earth will be judged. In past years I struggled to understand the purpose of believers going before the judgment seat of Christ. If our names are recorded in the Book of Life, why bother with judgment? Paul wrote that the judgment will reveal the nature of every person's work.

> *It will be revealed with fire, and the fire will*
> *test the quality of each man's work. If what he has*
> *built survives, he will receive his reward. If it is*
> *burned up, he will suffer loss; he himself will be*
> *saved, but only as one escaping through the flames.*
> (1 Cor. 3:13–15)

Suffer loss? What's that all about? I thought heaven was a happy place. Is it possible to feel regret in heaven? One Bible commentary suggests that this could mean that a person is not elevated to as high a rank and happiness as he otherwise would be. It also suggests that it shall be a detriment to him for all eternity, with the effects felt in all his residence in heaven—not producing misery but attending with him the consciousness that he might have been raised to superior bliss in the eternal abode. The actual phrase used is a law term that means "he shall be mulcted" or fined. His imperfections shall be removed and his salvation will be intact, but he may occupy a lower place in heaven.[1]

Ouch. We should keep in mind that commentaries differ in their interpretations of this passage, and there is no way to be certain what it means to "suffer loss."

Regardless, it certainly spurs you on to intentional living and makes you think twice about your motives in serving the Lord.

But let me interject an important consideration in the pursuit to leave a legacy that matters for eternity. If our motives in doing so are self-seeking or even for the sole benefit of others (even our husband and children), it may not survive the test of fire on Judgment Day. Our motive of the heart should be to bring glory and honor to God. Ironically, when we seek to please him, the rest will fall into place.

Scripture speaks specifically of crowns awarded to those who persevere under trial (James 1:12), shepherd God's flock (1 Pet. 5:2), and long for his return (2 Tim. 4:8). It also speaks of rewards given for our conduct (Ps. 62:12; Jer. 17:10; 32:19; Matt. 16:27). If in fact there is an awards day in heaven, I wonder how many Christians will face the sudden realization that they had their priorities in the wrong place while serving out their earthly tenure. Many who have served faithfully in the Lord's work may discover that they did so with the wrong motives and, therefore, forfeit an eternal reward. Should there be an awards day of sorts, we can all think of people who we feel certain will reap many crowns or rewards. Yet I wonder if it will be similar to the awards day at the end of my senior year, when the names of many who were virtual unknowns are called out. I am speaking of those whose works may have gone unnoticed by others while on earth, but be assured, they caught the eye of the Father.

I think of the countless missionaries who have given up everyday luxuries to relocate to foreign and sometimes hostile environments for the sake of Christ. Many have left their family and friends in order to share the love of

Christ with a lost and dying world. I think of the prayer warriors who are faithful to petition God behind the scenes. No request is too small, and they pray for many who will never know they are being prayed for. I think of a neighbor mom who lived down the street while I was growing up and invited me to church countless times. I think about the strength she exhibited when she was dying of cancer during my college years. Her silent example of godliness over the years planted seeds in my hardened heart and played a part in my decision to eventually become a Christian. Unfortunately, she died one year shy of my making that decision. I can't be sure she received a crown for her efforts, but I'm willing to bet God opened up the curtains of heaven and allowed her a glimpse of me surrendering my heart to Christ on that day in 1985.

I wonder if there will be a conscious awareness of regret, as some commentaries suggest, when we go before the judgment seat of Christ. If there is, my regret would not come at the thought of leaving the ceremony empty-handed with nothing to display on the mantel in my heavenly mansion. The crowns are not ours to keep. Revelation 4:10–11 speaks of the purpose of crowns or rewards we might receive:

> *The twenty-four elders fall down before him*
> *who sits on the throne, and worship him who lives*
> *for ever and ever. They lay their crowns before the*
> *throne and say:*
> *"You are worthy, our Lord and God,*
> *to receive glory and honor and power,*
> *for you created all things,*
> *and by your will they were created*
> *and have their being." (Rev. 4:10–11)*

Wow! If I don't have anything to lay at the feet of my Savior on that day, I will suffer loss. It won't be from envy of watching others lay their crowns at his feet in reverence and humility, but from sheer regret that I have nothing to offer him on that day to show my gratitude. I want to live my life in preparation for that day.

Leaving a Legacy that Matters

Some years ago my grandparents asked their four children to come for a discussion. Both grandparents were in their eighties and wanted to discuss their wills. They are both committed Christians and confident of their eternal home in heaven, so this was not an uncomfortable exercise. They discussed details, such as who would get the land, their home, and many other belongings.

As I pondered the thought of leaving possessions behind to loved ones, I began to think of the many things people leave as an inheritance. I reflected on a day I had visited my grandparents' home. My grandmother had been diagnosed for a second time with cancer and wanted to share a timely verse with me. As she opened her worn Bible and turned the pages, I could see the margins filled with her notes. The pages were so worn from the turning that they were falling out. As she read the verse to me, I found myself thinking, *Dear God, may my Bible be as weathered and worn as my grandmother's.*

Praise be to God—shortly before her death, she was able to read the above testament to her faith in *The Virtuous Woman Bible Study*. She wept, unable to grasp the power of a godly legacy now being lived out in the life of her once wayward granddaughter. As she hugged me tightly, she finally spoke and said, "I want you to have my

Bible." Today her Bible sits on the shelf in my office as a reminder of her legacy of faith. Sometimes when I miss her, I take it off the shelf and leaf gently through the pages. Tucked inside, undisturbed and exactly where she left it, is an *Open Windows* devotional turned to the last page she had read before entering the hospital just days before her death. I am comforted by her notes in the margins that, most likely, inspired her to deeper faith over the years. Many of the underlined verses give insight to her weaknesses. I was encouraged to see that she had struggles just like everyone else, but had taken them straight to the throne of grace. I have wondered how many times she turned these same pages, searching for a verse of encouragement during the season of her life when three of her four children were prodigals. She would see all of them return to the Lord well before her death.

I have wondered how many times she opened these same pages seeking wisdom in how best to reach the oldest grandchild who claimed not to believe in God. Yet God was faithful and drew that grandchild to him in a mighty way and, of all places, at a college retreat sponsored by my grandmother's very own church! That grandchild was me. To this day I vividly remember standing in line at a pay phone the following morning at the Baptist encampment with a quarter in hand, waiting to call her and tell her the good news. When she answered the phone, I told her that her prayers had been answered—the night before my name had been inscribed in the Lamb's Book of Life. She wept upon hearing the news and rushed out to buy me a brand-new study Bible to replace the children's Bible she and my grandfather had given me for Christmas at the age of ten. Both Bibles now sit on a shelf in my office next to my grandmother's priceless Bible. They are a reminder of my godly heritage and the responsibility I have to leave the same godly legacy to those who come behind me.

I, too, want to leave a legacy that matters for eternity. I want to be remembered as someone who refused to settle for average. I'm aiming high, and I'm not ashamed to say that I want to be a woman who excels them all. Though it is a daunting task, I will persevere in the pursuit—not for my own sake but because it pleases the Father. It's the very least I can do—after all he has done!

In the end, above all else, I want to bow in reverence before him, casting any crown I might receive at his feet and say, "You are worthy, our Lord and God, to receive glory and honor and power." Help me to live my entire life for that moment.

Conclusion

At the writing of this conclusion, this book is just shy of going to print, and I have just returned from a photo shoot for the front cover. While there, my editor handed the manuscript back to me for one final read-through and assigned me the task of writing a short conclusion. I knew that in order to wrap the book up in a few short pages, it would be necessary to read it through in one sitting. As luck would have it, I had a long layover in the airport that evening while waiting for my return flight home, so I found an unoccupied cluster of chairs tucked away in the corner of my gate and quickly established a makeshift office. I pulled out my manuscript, tuned out my surroundings, and began to read. It had been almost a year since I had written the initial chapters and much of the material seemed fresh, yet at the same time, familiar. As I read page after page, detailing the resumé of the virtuous woman, I felt somewhat conflicted. I vacillated back and forth between confidence and conviction as I measured my own progress against the Proverbs 31 woman's standard of virtue.

As I sat there in that airport in Nashville, I wrestled with the thought that as the author of a book on the virtuous woman, for heaven's sakes, I should have it all together in the virtue department. "Great," I thought. "I have only a few months to get my act together before this book hits the bookshelves!" As I continued reading, the enemy began to do a number on me—and the more I read, the worse it got. As I turned page after page, my eyes filled with tears as he whispered "hypocrite" in my ear, over and over again.

Now, don't misunderstand me here—I don't smoke, drink, or go out with my girlfriends on the weekends and dance on tables. I vote and pay my taxes like a good American citizen. I go to church every Sunday and I tithe off my book royalties. Occasionally, I will even let the person behind me with two items in the super market checkout line go in front of me, instead of averting my eyes and pretending not to notice. Unfortunately, my mental inventory of good deeds didn't seem to be enough to drown out the enemy's reminders. "What about all the 'taco nights' your poor family had to suffer through in order to meet this book deadline?" "What would the readers say if they knew your Sunday school class felt so sorry for you and your family that they brought you meals for two weeks?" "Would they read the book if they knew you wear a tankini to the swimming pool instead of a high-necked skirted one piece swimsuit? Is that virtuous?" "What about that day when your son was stranded in the school parking lot? Yep, you were so busy writing the chapter on 'looking well to the ways of your household' that you forgot that the poor kid got out early for final exams." "What would they say if they knew there were some nights when you were so tired from writing about being virtuous that you fell into the bed and gave your poor husband the 'touch me and prepare to die' look?" Over and over again these seeds of doubt were planted in my mind and made me wonder if I had misread the call God had placed on my heart to write this book.

And then something amazing happened. As my flight was announced and I stood in line to board the plane, my thoughts of inadequacy were interrupted when a young woman turned to me and asked if I had been the keynote speaker at a women's event that she had attended months prior in my hometown of Austin, Texas. I confirmed that I had been the speaker and as we talked further, she shared that she had initially been hesitant to attend the event, but that in the end, God had used it to mark a new beginning in her life. And then she thanked me for my willingness to share with an open heart. As my eyes filled with tears, this time for a different reason, I thought, "Isn't that just like God to show up and remind us of how far we've come when the enemy is beating us over the head with how far we have to go?"

There is no denying that the pursuit to be a virtuous woman is a daunting task. Yet, it is not God's desire that we turn the last page of this book feeling overwhelmed and depressed. Part of shattering the super woman myth will be acknowledging that we are not perfect. Try as we may, we will not be perfect until the day we stand before God, the almighty Author of virtue. I said this in the beginning and I will say it again: "God does not expect perfection, but rather perseverance." Please know that my prayer for you is this: As you persevere in the quest to be a virtuous woman, may God shower you with grace and mercy every step of the way and remind you often of how far you have come in the pursuit.

Endnotes

Chapter 1

1. Conversations between Adrian Rogers and Dale McCleskey.

Chapter 2

1. Media's Effects on Girls: Body Image and Gender Identity, Fact Sheet.

2. Laurie Mintz, lead author of the study and an associate professor of educational and counseling psychology at University Missouri-Columbia; ABCNews.com, 30 October 2002 (http://abc news.go.com/sections/living/healthology/HSsupermodel_ depressionon021029.html).

3. http://www.purdueexponent.org/2000/07/19/opinions/ body.html; *Eating Disorders Awareness Week* publication.

4. http://www.applesforhealth.com/neversatisf1.html.

5. Kenneth Osbeck, *101 Hymn Stories* (Grand Rapids, Mich: Kregel Publishers, 1982).

6. Taken from Corrie ten Boom's sermon, "Not Good if Detached," 1957.

Chapter 4

1. *Jamieson-Fausset-Brown Bible Commentary.* Electric text and markup, copyright 1999 by Epiphany Software.

Chapter 5

1. http://www.gospelcom.net/chi/DAILYF/2003/04/daily 04-15-2003.shtml.

2. Paul Lee Tan, *Encyclopedia of 7700 Illustrations* (Assurance Publishers, 1982) as quoted on BibleBelievers.com (http://www.biblebelievers.com/titanic.html).

3. Ibid.

Chapter 6

1. *Matthew Henry's Bible Knowledge Commentary* (from Bible Explorer 3 software). Underlying source materials. © 1983, by Scripture Press Publications, Inc. Licensed by Victor Books. Database © 2003 WORDsearch Corp.

2. "It Is Well with My Soul," Glimpses, Christian History Institute (http://www.gospelcom.net/chi/GLIMPSEF/Glimpses/glmps064.shtml).

3. "It Is Well," At The Well, (http://www.atthewell.com/itiswell/index.php).

Chapter 8

1. *Matthew Henry's Commentary on the Whole Bible* (from Bible Explorer 3 software). Electronic text and markup, copyright 1999 by Epiphany Software.

2. *Merriam-Webster Dictionary of Law,* © 1996 Merriam-Webster, Inc., s.v. "hearsay."

Chapter 9

1. J. Vernon McGee, *Thru the Bible* (Nashville, Tenn.: Thomas Nelson, 2002), Bible Explorer 3 software.

Chapter 10

1. David and Teresa Ferguson, *Intimate Encounters, Revised Edition* (Austin, Tex.: Relationship Press, 2001). Information concerning their workshops can be found at www.greatcommandment.net.

2. Lynn Okagaki, in Shelvia Dancy, "You've Got to Spell it out for Kids," 12 August 2000 (http://www.beliefnet.com/story/36/story_3672_1.html).

3. Ibid.

Chapter 11

1. Trent C. Butler, ed. *Holman Bible Dictionary* (Nashville, Tenn.: Broadman & Holman, 1991).

2. *New Unger's Bible Dictionary,* rev. ed. (Chicago, Ill.: Moody Press, 1988), 404.

3. Ibid.

Chapter 12

1. *Matthew Henry's Commentary* (from Bible Explorer 3 software). Electronic text and markup, copyright 1995 by Epiphany Software.